National Economic Development Offic

Shirts in the Seventies

A study of the strategic future of the United Kingdom shirt industry

Prepared by W S Atkins and Partners for the
Economic Development Committee for the
Clothing Industry

London, Her Majesty's Stationery Office, 1970

The Economic Development Committees are composed of
representatives of the three parties involved in industrial and
economic development—management, trade unions and government.
Their secretariat is provided by the National Economic Development
Office which is an independent, publicly financed body. This report
has been prepared by W S Atkins and Partners for the Clothing EDC,
under the guidance of the Shirt Industry Study Group. For
administrative convenience the booklet is printed and published
through HMSO.

National Economic Development Office
Millbank Tower, 21/41 Millbank
London S W 1
01–834 3811
September 1970

SBN 11 700517 7

Clothing EDC

Shirt Industry Study Group/List of Members

Chairman

N F Sussman, Director, L S and J Sussman Ltd

Members

A G R Gater, National Economic Development Office

M B Gluck, Chairman and Joint Managing Director, Rael-Brook Ltd

J T Holden, Honorary Member of the Executive Council of the Shirt Collar and Tie Manufacturers Federation

L A Matthews, JP, Assistant General Secretary, National Union of Tailors and Garment Workers

W K Pryke, Ministry of Technology

K F Pullum, Chairman, R H and S Rogers Ltd

J Rylands, Managing Director, Humphrey Lloyd and Sons Ltd

C V Syms, Assistant Marketing Manager – Retail, ICI Fibres Ltd

Secretary

Miss E M Wales, National Economic Development Office

Clothing EDC/List of members

Chairman

R Appleby, CBE, Chairman, Black and Decker Ltd

Members

W E Aston, Chairman and Managing Director, Wearwell Overall Co Ltd

A G R Gater, National Economic Development Office

D I Goldstone, JP, Chairman and Managing Director, The Sterling Rubber Co Ltd

J Gratwick, Managing Director, Urwick Orr and Partners

R D H Harmer, Chairman and Managing Director, F W Harmer and Co Ltd

F C Henry, OBE, JP, General Secretary, The Waterproof Garment Workers' Trade Union

S Kenton, Managing Director, Simon Kenton Ltd

J Lee, Managing Director, (Retired), Julian Lee Ltd

J Macgougan, General Secretary, National Union of Tailors and Garment Workers

L A Matthews, JP, Assistant General Secretary, National Union of Tailors and Garment Workers

P L McConnell, Director, Kayser Bondor Ltd

J H McEnery, Ministry of Technology

S R Rawson, Managing Director, Prices Tailors Ltd

J Steinberg, Chairman and Joint Managing Director, Steinberg and Sons Ltd

N F Sussman, Director, L S and J Sussman Ltd

Miss E Sutton, Industrial Officer, National Union of Tailors and Garment Workers

Secretary

C Leach, National Economic Development Office

Preface

In January 1970 a study of major importance to the Clothing Industry, *Your future in clothing,* was published. This report, which was sponsored by the Clothing EDC and prepared by Associated Industrial Consultants Ltd, gives an outline of the market opportunities up to 1978 in 19 different sectors of the Clothing Industry, taking into consideration such factors as trends in consumer expenditure, imports and exports, projected increases in wages and other costs, and potential increases in productivity.

It has always been the intention of the Clothing EDC that this report should be the first stage of its work of helping different sectors of the industry to improve their economic performance. The function of *Your future in clothing* was essentially that of mapping out the future environment in which the industry would operate and its scope did not include making specific recommendations for action by individual firms and the industry's organisations. The second stage of the work was seen as depth studies into those areas most affected by the changes forecast in *Your future in clothing.*

The study of the UK shirt industry was the first of these follow-up studies to be initiated as at an early stage in the work for *Your future in clothing* it became apparent that imported shirts already accounted for a significant proportion of the total UK market. It was therefore decided to sponsor a study on the UK Shirt Industry and a study group composed of representatives of the industry was set up under the chairmanship of Mr Norman Sussman. W S Atkins and Partners were commissioned to undertake the project.

The study is the first objective attempt to assess the industry, its environment and the future opportunities open to its members. I am sure that it will be an important and constructive stimulus to all those interested in the future prosperity of the industry. I hope that all manufacturers will read it and take the opportunity of testing their views against the information and recommendations set out in the report.

Finally I would like to thank Mr Norman Sussman, the Chairman of the study group which guided the project. His enthusiasm and leadership played a very large part in ensuring the success of this study.

Robert Appleby, Chairman, Clothing EDC

Foreword

In the past fifteen years the shirt industry has been faced with many problems. Such changes as the introduction of new fabrics, greater attention to styling and an increasing shortage of labour have exposed the need for considerable investment — both to increase productivity and to provide an attractive working environment. However, investment results from confidence in the future and the threat of rising imports from overseas made this difficult to maintain.

The threat first appeared in 1953 when nearly 1½ million shirts were imported from Hong Kong alone. By 1963 over 15 million shirts were being imported, and at the same time Portugal began to be a significant exporter of nylon shirts to this country.

The Shirt Collar and Tie Manufacturers Federation had made representations to the Government as early as 1954, but at that time there was no readily available evidence to substantiate their case. In 1968, however, the EDC asked AIC to undertake a study on the future markets for the Clothing Industry, and information on the shirt sector brought to light in the early months of the study confirmed manufacturers' fears. After consulting representatives of the industry, the EDC decided therefore to launch a study on the shirt industry and accordingly a study group was set up, the members of which represented major aspects of the industry. W S Atkins and Partners were chosen to carry out the study and their terms of reference were as follows:

"The objective of the study is to ensure a satisfactory level of economic activity and financial performance in the changing environment of the future. The study will specifically consider the international competitiveness of the industry and will indicate favourable policies for five years ahead. Information and recommended actions will be set out for the industry as a whole in such a way that these can be incorporated and implemented by individual firms. Actions or initiatives on the part of Government which can have a major effect on the future of the industry will be outlined."

Financial approval for the study (which has cost over £16,000) was dependent on the industry, or those associated with it, contributing 25 per cent of the cost, and the fact that this sum was readily forthcoming is further confirmation of the concern that was felt for the industry's future.

I would like to thank the consultants involved on the project who undertook the work of the study in a very professional manner, the staff of the National Economic Development Office and my colleagues on the study group who whilst not necessarily endorsing all the views of the consultants provided the medium of full and frank discussion on every matter arising from the report. My thanks are also due to the Chairman of the Clothing EDC, Robert Appleby, whose initiative and enthusiasm were largely responsible for this project being initiated. Finally I would like to acknowledge generous contributions to the cost of the study made by the following organisations:

Carrington and Dewhurst	Marks and Spencer
Coats Patons	The Shirt Collar and Tie Manufacturers Federation
Dubin Haskell Jacobson	Singer Sewing Machine Company
English Calico	Staflex International
Hoechst UK	Texifused
ICI Fibres	Trubenised

It was their support, inspired by their faith in the industry's future prosperity which made this report possible.

Norman Sussman, Chairman, Shirt Industry Study Group

Contents

Part 2 — The current environment Page

Part 3 — Prospects for the future

List of tables

List of illustrations

Introduction

The study was commissioned at the end of June 1969 and was carried out during the period July to December of that year, and involved some 16 man months of effort. However, in order to take advantage of figures relating to the whole of 1969, the work was not finalised until June 1970. Whilst the recommendations of the study are based on analysis of available facts, they also rely on subjective judgements. In making such judgements, it is emphasised that the prime responsibility for the conclusion drawn rests with the consultants, although they received invaluable guidance from the Study Group.

The scope of the study allowed little opportunity for the collection of new information on an industry wide basis, and in the main data was obtained from a number of recognised sources, to which reference is made in the text. They were the Ministry of Technology Business Monitor, HM Customs and Excise returns on imports and exports, the recently published National Board for Prices and Incomes report on Pay and Conditions in the Clothing Manufacturing Industries, and the Department of Employment and Productivity figures on labour statistics. In addition, ICI Fibres Ltd made available the results of their continuous market survey on the UK shirt market, and reference was made to two Clothing EDC reports, *Attainable production targets** published in 1969, and produced by Kurt Salmon and PE Associates Ltd, and *Your future in clothing*† produced by Associated Industrial Consultants Ltd and published in January 1970. Other official bodies to whom reference on specific matters was made included the Shirt, Collar and Tie Manufacturers Federation, the National Union of Tailors and Garment Workers, the Shirt Federation of Northern Ireland, and the Clothing and Textile Institutes and the Textile Council. Information on specific aspects of the shirt business was also obtained during some 50 visits made to interested parties in Great Britain. These contacts were selected, with the assistance of the Study Group, on the basis of their being likely to contribute valid information and comment in their own particular areas of activity. They included suppliers of raw material, machinery makers, woven and knitted cloth producers, merchants and importers, shirt manufacturing companies of various sizes, and retail outlets representative of the main channels of shirt distribution in the UK.

Information on various aspects of overseas activity was derived from visits to four selected countries, the number of contacts made in each being as follows:

United States of America	14
West Germany	17
Portugal	13
Sweden	6

These contacts were made with the co-operation of the Study Group, assisted by the Ministry of Technology and the Embassies concerned.

We wish to acknowledge the great help and co-operation received from our sources of information, from official bodies, from companies in the UK shirt industry or associated with it, and from overseas organisations.

---

*Attainable production targets, 1969, HMSO 22s 6d
†Your future in clothing, 1970, HMSO 15s

Our thanks are due to the members of the Study Group, both in their capacity as individual members of the Committee and as representatives of various organisations associated with the industry. Finally, we wish to thank the staff of the National Economic Development Office, who, in providing the central administration for the Study, gave us much direct help.

The study was carried out by the following consultants of W S Atkins & Partners:

Project leader A G J Baker

J E Moore

W J Parker

Additional support was provided by other members of the Planning Division of the Company under the overall control of E M Lewis, the Director in charge of Planning.

Summary and recommendations

The text of the report is divided into three parts, which deal in turn with the situation over the past ten years, the present environment and the prospects up to 1975 as they relate to the UK shirt industry.

The review of the current situation of the UK industry reveals the following picture:

The total market for shirts has shown a steady increase in both volume and value terms for a number of years, with a rate of growth slightly higher than that of clothing as a whole.

The proportion of the total UK market taken by imports has not increased in volume terms over the past 10 years, despite significant fluctuations from year to year. 28 per cent of all shirts sold in the UK are imported and these are largely at the cheaper end of the market, although the medium and higher priced market sectors are presently coming under pressure from imports.

The UK industry is very fragmented, as a result of its long entrepreneurial tradition, and the fact that it is not highly capital intensive.

The profitability of the firms in the industry varies considerably but the larger companies seem better able to avoid making a loss. For an industry with the level of risk associated with the shirt business, the average profitability seems low.

Shirt manufacturing costs in the UK would be higher than those of overseas countries with lower labour costs, even if all possible improvements in productivity were made. Thus the UK industry can only compete effectively in those areas of the market where manufacturing costs are not the decisive factor.

Managers of shirt companies tend to be production rather than marketing oriented. The promotion of branded merchandise is less intense than in other large consumer markets, although significant compared with other sectors of the clothing industry.

This analysis of the current situation shows that although the UK suffers certain disadvantages compared to some overseas producers, notably the level of production costs, there also seem to be other inherent weaknesses in industry structure and marketing approach which have led to the UK industry surrendering a large part of the initiative to its customers and suppliers. Seen in the light of these disadvantages, the pessimistic forecasts of a shirt market growth of only 2-2½ per cent per annum, largely taken by imports, as in *Your future in clothing,* seems justified if no concerted action is taken.

On the other hand, the home industry has potential advantages which could be exploited if the industry changes its approach. The industry's proximity to the market, for example, allows for frequent and informal contact between suppliers and customers. In the past, the shirt market has shown itself responsive to the introduction of new fabrics and fashion ideas, and the increasing fashion awareness among consumers gives further opportunities in this direction. This has led to the following major recommendations:

The UK industry should adopt a more aggressive marketing policy, with the objective of influencing the home market in a way which will place the home manufacturer at maximum advantage. Defensive strategies based on protective tariffs and quotas would not be in the interests of the industry, even if they were acceptable to the Government, as it would delay necessary change. A suggested method is the creation of some degree of syndicated fashion, by which an emphasis on selected colours, designs and styles would be presented by the industry leaders, to provide a focal point for UK marketing effort and make it more difficult for overseas manufacturers to compete. Branded manufacturers will need to increase their expenditure on promotion to around 6 per cent of their total turnover.

An information system should be set up by the industry as a whole, to provide background data against which individual companies can develop their plans.

UK companies must do more corporate planning. Growth will bring benefits provided that organisations make a comprehensive assessment of their position in the total market, and individual companies should plan all their activities accordingly. Increased promotional spending and changes in selling techniques will also be necessary.

Companies must improve productivity and reduce costs with the utmost vigour. Big improvements in efficiency are possible by the application of modern techniques of production and workplace engineering.

Despite the relatively good industrial relations which have existed, changes will be necessary. With the advent of equal pay.for women and the rapid movement of wages, and as firms become bigger, relations will become more formalised, and management and unions must ensure that the present degree of understanding and co-operation is maintained.

The industry will need to devote more effort to training for management and staff at all levels.

In order to implement these changes capital investment of about £14 million will be required by the industry during the period considered. There should be no problems attracting this in view of the improved profit performance which it is believed the industry of the future can achieve.

If the aggressive policy outlined for the industry as a whole and for individual companies is followed, the study predicts that by 1975

The market will grow at the rate of between 4 and 5 per cent, in volume terms per year leading to a UK production of about 71 million units compared to current production of 54 million units.

About four large firms will emerge, each with a turnover approaching £10 million per year. The total number of firms in the industry will be reduced from about 250 to about 150.

Improvements in productivity will be accompanied by a reduction in the work force of about 18 per cent, this should not however cause any general problems of redundancy.

The alternative pattern of decline for the UK shirt industry is spelled out in *Your future in clothing.* It is strongly felt that the shrinking role of the home manufacturers can be reversed by strong and vigorous action, and that the responsibility for this initiative lies with the industry itself.

Definitions and assumptions

The following assumptions have been used throughout the Report, except where stated to the contrary.

Definition of the industry
The shirt industry is taken to include manufacturers of all formal and informal classes of men's and boys' shirts regardless of their construction and fabric, including manufacturers of leisure shirts of light weight fabric, but not the collarless tee-shirt of knitted cotton which is mainly produced overseas.

Value of the pound
The value of the pound sterling is taken as that ruling in mid 1969. Financial statistics for earlier years have been uplifted by the following multiplying factors to allow for inflation:

1969	1968	1967	1966	1965	1964	1963	1962	1961	1960
1.00	1.03	1.06	1.10	1.14	1.17	1.21	1.25	1.29	1.33

All costs, prices, taxes, tariffs and rates of exchange are taken at their levels prevailing in mid 1969.

Conversion and comprehensive conversion costs
In those parts of the Report dealing with process cost comparisons, reference is made to comprehensive conversion cost. The concept of comprehensive cost is very useful for decision making, but the term is not widely used in the industry, and some definition is therefore required.

The 'conversion cost' of a process can be considered as built up from the costs of labour, consumable materials, maintenance materials, fuel and power, and overheads. However, it does not include the cost of capital involved or the profit expected. For decision making purposes it is convenient to regard capital as a commodity which is hired for an annual charge, this charge taking into account the requirements of depreciation, taxation, interest, dividends and retained profits. By adding to the conversion cost of a process the charges on the capital employed, a new and all embracing figure is obtained by which alternative processes can be realistically compared. This new figure is termed the 'comprehensive conversion cost'. It should be noted that the charge is only applied to capital required for new plant. Existing plant and other assets for which capital has irretrievably been committed must be treated as a heritage which exists whatever new strategy is adopted.

For the purpose of this Report, the charge to be made on capital in a non-development area has been decided upon as a minimum of 20 per cent per year. After allowing for the delays between spending the capital and achieving a normal year's profit, and after allowing for the expected commercial life of a project, this figure corresponds (see Appendices C and D) to a discounted cash flow (DCF) rate of 10 per cent per year before the payment of Corporation Tax, taken to be at the rate of 45 per cent. The 10 per cent DCF rate corresponds roughly to the general opportunity level of investment in British industry at present.

Conversion and comprehensive costs are used in this Report only for the purpose of comparing production alternatives. The costs may not include certain overheads or cost recoveries which are reckoned to be the same for each alternative. For this reason the costs should not be used for establishing pricing policies; nor can they be compared with costs in individual companies.

Establishments

For the purposes of the study, an establishment is defined as a separate production unit having a distinct postal address; it may be a department, branch or subsidiary company in its own right, but is an identifiable unit from the point of view of shirt manufacture.

Use of log scale on diagrams

In many diagrams appearing in this report the horizontal or vertical axes have been drawn to a log scale. This means that the proportional increase between figures shown on the axes is constant.

Part 1   The situation up to the present

Chapter 1   The market

From the best data available, the number of shirts sold in the UK in 1969 is estimated as 71 million and the total value of retail shirt sales as £138 million. Since 1960 the market has grown at an average annual rate of 3.6 per cent in volume and at 4.2 per cent in value – higher rates than for clothing as a whole.

Retail selling prices in real terms have remained almost constant but selling prices at the time rose significantly between 1963 and 1966, the period of rapid growth in nylon shirt sales.

1.1 Total size

Basic information on the size of the UK home shirt market was derived from two sources, the Ministry of Technology and ICI Fibres Limited. In the quinquennial Censuses of Production, the Ministry of Technology Business Statistics Office collects information on the value and quantity of sales by establishments with 25 or more employees. This information is supplemented by the figures collected quarterly by Mintech and published in the Business Monitor of sales, both value and quantity by establishments with 100 or more employees. This quarterly information can be adjusted by coverages estimated from the 1963 Census of Production to give estimates of sales of all establishments employing 25 or more persons. These total sales estimates assume that the firms retain the same market share as in the census, that is the method can take no account of firms' declining or increasing shares or of firms leaving or entering the industry. Thus, whilst the data on the larger firms is reasonably accurate, the total output figure is only an estimate. In an expanding economy the figures tend, it is thought, to under-estimate the total volume of home production. As the Mintech data relates to total home production, additional statistics on imports and exports are necessary to ascertain the size of the UK total market, and these are available from H M Customs and Excise.

ICI Fibres' information is obtained from a continual consumer survey. Individual purchasers are interviewed on a weekly basis to discover the frequency and type of their purchases of all types of garments in order to provide the company with the pattern of demand for its own and its competitors' fibres. The data on shirts is derived from the results of some 1700 interviews each year. There is a tendency for surveys based on this type of interview to over-estimate the size and value of a market sector, due to subjective factors, but they can be invaluable in revealing changes in the market situation, both in overall terms and in the breakdown of the market by, for example, fibre type and garment retail price.

It is interesting to note that the Ministry of Technology and ICI Fibres data coincided (in quantity terms) in 1963, the year of the last Census of Production for which detailed results are available, though there has been some divergence since that date. Other sources of basic information on the shirt market size used in this Report include unpublished estimates by the larger manufacturers and leading retail outlets, and figures of shirt manufacturing companies filed with the Registrar of Companies.

From all sources the number of shirts sold in 1969 has been estimated as 71 million, and the total value of retail sales (assuming manufacturers' selling prices to be some 60 per cent of the retail selling price, including purchase tax of 13.75 per cent) as £138 million. (Both the Ministry of Technology and ICI Fibres figures are basically concerned with numbers of shirts, although in each case, estimates of corresponding prices are given, these prices being at the manufacturers' selling price level in the Ministry of Technology data and at the retail level in the ICI Fibres data).

This estimate comes between the corresponding Ministry of Technology and ICI Fibres figures as shown in the table below, and is rather closer to the latter data as the Ministry of Technology values do not take account of the output of shirt manufacturing companies employing fewer than 25 persons. In deriving the import figures from the published Customs and Excise statistics, a factor of 33 per cent has been added to the value of the imported goods to allow for duty and distribution costs at the manufacturers' selling price level.

The corresponding figures for the total UK shirt market in 1969 from the Ministry of Technology (and Customs and Excise) and ICI Fibres are as follows:

	Total retail sales value £ millions	Number of shirts sold Millions
Ministry of Technology (with Customs and Excise import/export data)	107	60
ICI Fibres	155	76

The estimate of sales in 1969 of 71 million shirts is believed to provide a valid basis for this Report, even though no use of the (unpublished) 1968 Census of Production figures figures has been possible, as half the relevant companies have not yet filed their returns. It does not compare directly with the estimates made in the Clothing EDC study entitled *Your future in clothing** for 1968, being a further refinement based on a more detailed analysis, of the available information on the shirt sector of the clothing industry, and taking 1969 figures into account.

1.2 Growth

In an evaluation of a given market, information on its rate of development and on changes in consumer demands is perhaps even more important than statistics on its current size. Figures 1.1 and 1.2 show the development of the UK shirt market over the past 10 years. (This information is also presented in Appendix F).

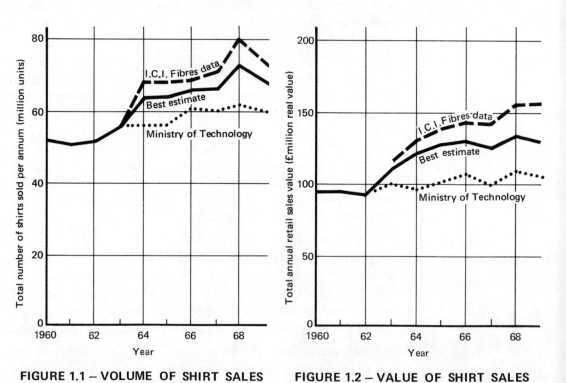

FIGURE 1.1 – VOLUME OF SHIRT SALES IN THE UK

FIGURE 1.2 – VALUE OF SHIRT SALES IN THE UK

*Your future in clothing, 1970, HMSO price 15s

4

All the available sources provide evidence of growth in recent years. Although the growth pattern shown by the Ministry of Technology statistics (as in Figures 1.1 and 1.2) is relatively low, being just under 2 per cent per year, the ICI Fibres' figures and independent estimates based on cloth purchases by the home shirt industry show growth rates in excess of 5 per cent per year. The best estimates based on the data shown in Figures 1.1 and 1.2 give an average annual growth rate of some 3.6 per cent in number of shirts produced and 4.2 per cent in real value terms. The growth rate in this period would appear to have well exceeded the growth rate for consumer expenditure on clothing as a whole, estimated between 1960 and 1968 at 2.3 per cent a year. This latter growth rate is marginally below that for total consumer spending, as derived from the National Income and Expenditure Blue Book 1969.

In the market statistics shown in Figures 1.1 and 1.2, the 1969 data has been extrapolated from the results of the first 9 months, assuming a similar seasonal variation to previous years. The fact that the earlier parts of 1969 were in general periods of uncertainty among retailers, owing largely to the current opinion of the overall economic situation in the country, may have contributed to the apparent fall in the market size from the peak in 1968. Several individual shirt manufacturers are known to have recorded excellent results in the fourth quarter of 1969, and the consolidated figures for the year may prove to be slightly higher than the estimates given in Figures 1.1 and 1.2 as a result.

The pattern of retail shirt prices for the same period based on the best market estimates is shown below:

Table 1.1   Average retail selling price of shirts on the UK market

Year	1960	1961	1962	1963	1964	1965	1966	1967	1968	1969
Average retail price (s d) (1969 value)	35/7	37/3	36/0	38/7	38/0	40/0	39/10	37/5	37/3	38/9
Actual retail price (s d) (at the time)	26/9	28/10	28/10	32/0	32/4	35/3	36/0	35/3	36/3	38/9

There was a marked rise in the average retail selling price during the period of the rapid growth of the warp knitted nylon garment (1963–1966). That it has not been sustained, despite the recent tendency of the average work content of the home produced garments to increase, is largely due to the influx of cheaper imported shirts.

Chapter 2 United Kingdom trade

In 1969, 51 million home-produced shirts, with a retail value of £115 million, were sold in the UK; 3 million were exported. Since 1960 UK production has grown at 3.3 per cent per year by volume, retail prices being between 13–18 per cent above those of all shirts sold over the period. Imports have risen but kept the same proportion of the home market; Portugal in 1969 displaced Hong Kong as the biggest source of imports.

International trade in shirts and fabrics is subject to tariffs and quotas, the UK at present being relatively well protected against imports. About 30 per cent of all cotton fabric used by the home industry is imported but over 90 per cent of warp knitted nylon is produced in the UK.

2.1 United Kingdom production of shirts

Home production is the main source of shirts sold to the UK consumer. In 1969, about 51 million of the 71 million shirts sold were produced at home, some 3 million UK produced shirts being exported: the retail value of these home-produced shirts sold in the UK was some £115 million.

Taking a best estimate between the ICI Fibres and Ministry of Technology figures, supplemented by the Customs and Excise export statistics, home production rose in volume at an average rate of 3.3 per cent per year over the period 1960–1969, as shown in Figure 2.1

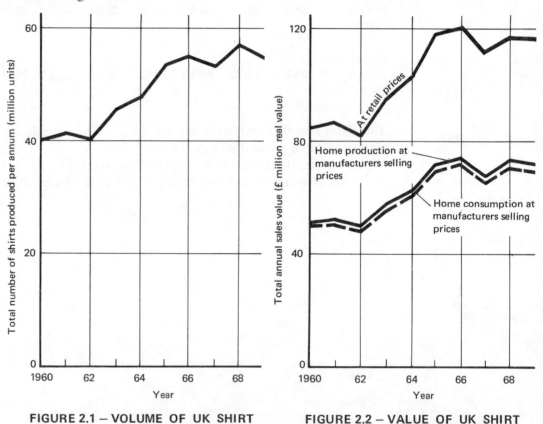

FIGURE 2.1 – VOLUME OF UK SHIRT PRODUCTION

FIGURE 2.2 – VALUE OF UK SHIRT PRODUCTION

Measured in 1969 constant prices, the average rise over the same period was 3.7 per cent per year, as shown below in Figure 2.2. (The information shown in those two figures is also shown in Appendix F). As before, it has been assumed that manufacturers' selling prices are, on average, some 60 per cent of the retail selling prices.

Thus, both in unit and in value terms, home production has achieved a reasonably steady growth record in recent years, even though total clothing expenditure, as a proportion of total consumer spending, has declined slightly in the last decade. The shirt manufacturers, imports apart, have slowly taken an increasing share, amounting in 1968 to about 15.5 per cent of the consumer expenditure on men's and boys' outerwear and innerwear, as reported in *Your future in clothing*.

The retail selling price of the home-produced shirts has varied little over the past nine years in real value, as shown in Table 2.1 below, although the actual selling price in the shops has risen by some 35 per cent over the same period, thus keeping very much in line with inflationary trends.

Table 2.1 Average retail selling price of home produced shirts

Year	1960	1961	1962	1963	1964	1965	1966	1967	1968	1969
Average retail price (s d) (1969 value)	43/3	42/7	41/10	43/3	44/0	45/0	44/7	42/10	42/0	43/6
Actual retail price (s d) (at the time)	32/5	33/0	33/5	35/10	37/7	39/8	40/7	40/3	40/10	43/6

2.2 Imports of shirts

Excluding knitted cotton garments, which being largely of the 'tee-shirt' type, are outside the scope of this study, the pattern of shirt imports, by quantity and value, is shown on Figures 2.3 and 2.4. This data is drawn from the Customs and Excise returns.

The general pattern of imports is one of a slow rise over the past ten years, with short term variations largely dependent on prevailing economic conditions and the appearance of new product types. For example, although there is no direct evidence, the very high level of largely woven cotton shirts imported in 1964 could have resulted from pressure by suppliers of these garments to increase sales in the face of the newly introduced warp knitted nylon shirts, which were becoming popular at that time.

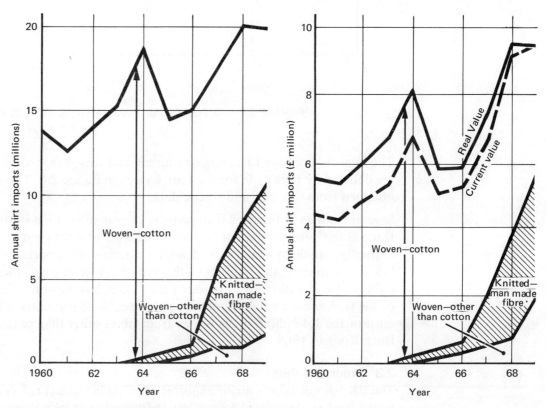

FIGURE 2.3 – VOLUME OF SHIRT IMPORTS
INTO THE UK

FIGURE 2.4 – VALUE OF SHIRT IMPORTS
INTO THE UK

The relatively rapid growth in the total level of imports during the period 1966–1968 was largely a result of the appearance of Portugal as a major low-cost producer of warp knitted nylon shirts, although the growth in nylon shirt imports was at the expense of the number of woven cotton garments entering the country. Together with the growth of nylon shirt imports over the past four years, there has been a steady though much less dramatic increase in the imports of garments woven from fibres other than cotton; these are largely blends of polyester with cotton or other man-made fibres.

The data on Figures 2.3 and 2.4 shows that the rapid rise in imports during 1966–1968 was not continued in 1969, when the import level in both number of units and value was virtually the same as in the previous year. Thus the immediate fear of the UK industry of a continued massive rise in imports has not been fulfilled. There was a noticeable rise in 1969 in the number of imported shirts made from fabric woven from fibres other than cotton over the 1968 figures; this was primarily due to the growth of imports of polyester/cotton shirts from Hong Kong.

As a proportion of the home market, imports have not changed significantly over the last ten years, as shown in Figure 2.5 below; fluctuations, in both quantity and value terms, have tended to even out over the years.

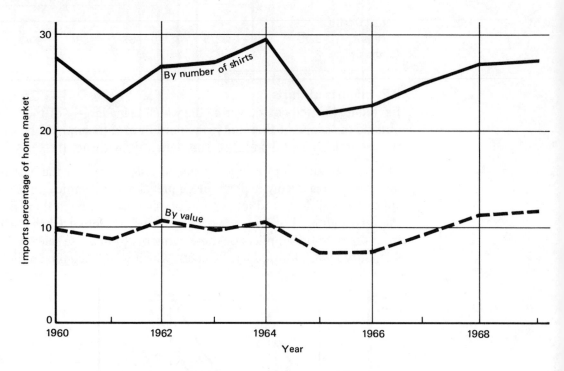

FIGURE 2.5 – IMPORTS AS PERCENTAGE OF UK MARKET

The imports from the three largest sources, and from other sources, selling into the UK are detailed by fibre type for the past 4 years in Figure 2.6. These figures were obtained from Customs and Excise data. .

Several features of Figure 2.6 are worthy of comment. First Portugal has replaced Hong Kong as the largest source of imports in number of units (and in value terms as well). Secondly, the slight resurgence of woven cotton shirt imports from Hong Kong in 1968 has not continued, and imports of this type from there have fallen from some 11.2 million to 6.3 million over the four years. There has, however, been some substitution of the traditional cotton imports by polyester blend garments, which accounted for most of the 1.4 million shirts woven from fibres other than cotton imported from Hong Kong in 1969.

2.3 Exports of shirts
The UK has not been a major exporter of shirts in the last ten years. Individual companies have made isolated forays into individual markets without capturing a large share of any one; and some have maintained a steady level of exports, with mixed

8

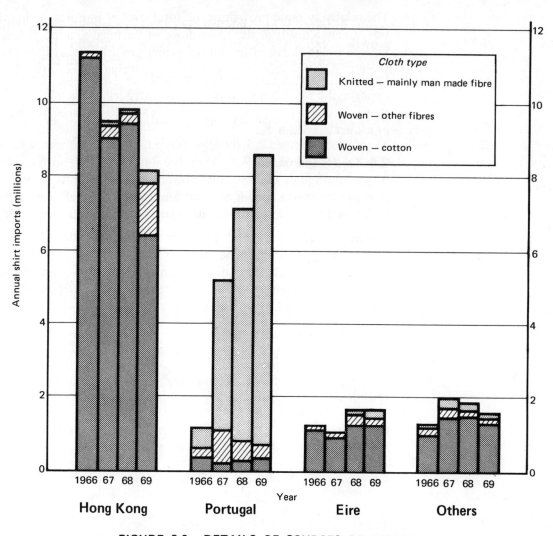

FIGURE 2.6 – DETAILS OF SOURCES OF IMPORTS

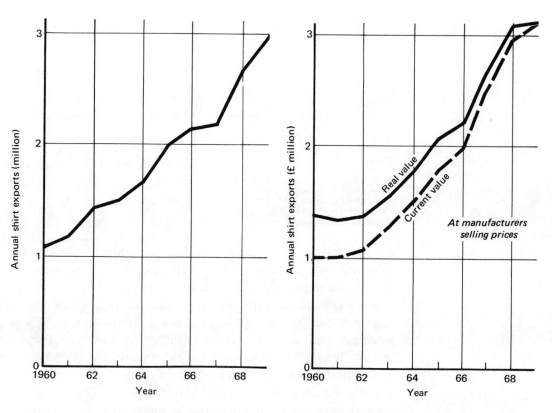

FIGURE 2.7 – VOLUME OF UK SHIRT EXPORTS

FIGURE 2.8 – VALUE OF SHIRT EXPORTS

results in terms of profitability. The Customs and Excise statistics show a steady growth in exports over the past five years, as shown in Figures 2.7 and 2.8; but even in 1969, exports amounted to only some 5.5 per cent of home production in quantity terms and some 2.7 per cent by value. These figures include some 350,000 knitted shirt exports; the total exported under this category is considerably higher, but many of these are of rather heavier construction and do not strictly conform to the definition of a shirt as used here.

2.4 Tariffs and quotas

A brief outline of present tariffs and quotas will help to explain the import and export position described above; detailed discussion of the effects on costs of trade restrictions is reserved for Chapter 6 where the UK's international competitiveness is analysed.

Tables 2.2 and 2.3 give the current international tariffs on shirts and shirt fabrics respectively for the countries that now concern the UK shirt industry or are likely to concern it within the next decade — namely, the UK itself, Portugal and Sweden (representing EFTA), the EEC (an entity for international trade purposes), and the USA.

Table 2.2   International tariffs—shirts

	100% cotton Current 1969	1/1/72	67/33 polyester/cotton Current 1969	1/1/72	Nylon Current 1969	1/1/72
UK						
Full rate	20%	20%	78d/lb or 23%*	20%	78d/lb or 23%*	20%
Commonwealth	FREE	17%	90% of above	90% of above	90% of above	90% of above
EFTA	FREE	FREE	FREE	FREE	FREE	FREE
Sweden						
EFTA	FREE	FREE	FREE	FREE	FREE	FREE
Others	15%	15%	15%	15%	13%	13%
EEC						
EEC	FREE	FREE	FREE	FREE	FREE	FREE
Others	19.3%	17%	19.3%	17%	19.3%	17%
USA						
MFN rate†	23%	21%	27.5%+ 25d/lb	27.5%+ 25d/lb	32.5%+ 25d/lb	32.5%+ 25d/lb

All duties % ad valorem or pence.

*Whichever is the greater.
†most favoured nation.

From Table 2.2 it is evident that, in international trade in made-up shirts, the UK is relatively well protected against imports, except those from other EFTA members and cotton shirts from the Commonwealth, for which a quota system operates at present. The USA, which is also in a relatively protected position, operates tariff control against imports from the Far East but has as yet no quotas for shirts or shirtings. In both countries, protection is marginally higher for man-made fibre than for cotton garments, apparently due to the influence of the man-made fibre producers in international textile markets. It is also noteworthy that the EEC is protected by a higher tariff than Sweden — a difference that will become less in 1972.

The import of woven cotton cloth and made-up woven cotton garments into the UK from Hong Kong is regulated by quota at present. The total woven cloth quota, which

Table 2.3 International tariffs—shirting fabrics

	100% cotton Current 1969	1/1/72	67/33 polyester/cotton Current 1969	1/1/72	Nylon Current 1969	1/1/72
UK			17½%+ 3.33d/lb		17½%+ 3½d/lb	
Full rate	17½%	17½%	or 5d/sq yd	4.8d/sq yd or 17½%*	or 7d/sq yd*	17½%
Commonwealth	FREE	15%	85% of above	85% of above	85% of above	85% of above
EFTA	FREE	FREE	FREE	FREE	FREE	FREE
Portugal† EFTA	4d/lb surcharge	††	373d/lb +4d/lb surcharge	††	424d/lb +4d/lb surcharge	††
MFN rate	109d/lb		934d/lb		708d/lb	
Sweden EFTA	FREE	FREE	FREE	FREE	FREE	FREE
Others	13%	13%	13%	13%	10%	10%
EEC EEC	FREE	FREE	FREE	FREE	FREE	FREE
Others	14%	14%	16.6%	16%	14%	13%
USA MFN rate	16.3% Typical shirting	13.7%	22.5%+ 20d/lb	22.5%+ 13d/lb	20%+ 25d/lb	20%+ 25d/lb

All duties % ad valorem of pence.

*Whichever is the greater.
†Drawback applies on re-export within EFTA.
††Future rates for Portugal are unknown owing to 10 year latitude allowed to adjust to GATT.

has been almost constant for the last three years, in 1969 was 190.6 million square yards cloth equivalent in which made-up shirts had their own component quota which is not published officially. However, in 1969 this quota of shirts was only 45 per cent utilised, demonstrating that the quota was not the limiting factor in that year on cotton shirt imports from Hong Kong.

Most fabric tariffs are up to 5 per cent less than for the corresponding shirts, to compensate for the added values in the made-up garment. Again the UK and the USA are well protected by comparison with EFTA and the EEC. Portugal at the moment has an effective tariff control to protect its fabric producers but is likely to be brought into line with the GATT recommendations in the not-too-distant future, although the 10-year latitude for adjustments will not encourage rapid amendments.

The quota for cotton fabric imports from Hong Kong into the UK has been filled in recent years, and this has led to competition among the Hong Kong merchants to participate in the quota, and hence to 'buy' themselves on to the quota, with a resulting increase in cost of the fabrics to the UK manufacturer. The actual effect of the tariff imposed on Commonwealth cotton fabric in 1972 will not therefore be as great as might at first appear.

Portugal, on the other hand, enjoys the tariff-free EFTA advantage over Hong Kong for nylon and polyester-cotton garments. Its tariff wall against manufactured fabric has led to a reverse trade from UK to Portugal in filament nylon which largely finds its way back to the UK as finished garments.

2.5 Cloth sources

In the case of woven cloths, there is fierce competition in the cheaper classes of product between the home textile trade and imported cloth, especially Hong Kong fabrics. In the better quality of woven cotton shirtings, the keenest competition comes from countries such as Austria, Switzerland and Italy, where in the opinion of most UK shirt manufacturers, suppliers combine excellence of design and colour with swift and reliable service for small orders. Thus the ratio between the quantities of imported and UK-woven cloth is sensitive at the cheap end of the market to tariffs and quota restrictions, and at the quality end to the requirements of the more fashion-conscious shirting buyer. The quality and value of woven polyester blends depend largely on the properties of the man-made fibres, and on the finishes, colours and designs available.So far, no firm pattern of quality has emerged, and the service which will be available to the home shirt industry in the future will depend largely on the activities of the major fibre suppliers concerned, both at home and abroad.

Almost the opposite situation applies to warp knitted nylon shirtings. Although the first commercial shirtings originated in Sweden in the early 1960s, the UK knitters have since invested heavily in production plant and in design expertise. This, added to the high level of interest of the main nylon supplier in this country, ICI Fibres Ltd., has led to UK leadership in the field; and now a large part of the warp knitted nylon shirting used by the UK shirt manufacturers is supplied by the home knitting trade.

Although no reliable and comprehensive data is available on the present proportion of shirting cloths of all types imported, the latest figures (for 1967) show that some 30 per cent (by weight) of all cotton fabric used by the home industry comes from overseas, whilst the proportion of warp knitted nylon cloths imported is less than some 10 per cent of the total home consumption.

Chapter 3   The United Kingdom shirt industry

The industry's structure is highly fragmented. The present 750 establishments are owned by some 250 separate companies, and, in spite of some groupings and links with outside organisations, 60 per cent of the home sales is supplied by independent companies, the largest group contributing only 12 per cent.

In 1968 the industry employed *37,000 people – 8.8 per cent of the total clothing labour force. About 85 per cent of establishments employed fewer than 100 people, and 46 per cent of workers were employed in such establishments; productivity rose with size of establishment. 92 per cent of workers were women. From 1960–68 the labour cost element of turnover declined by 7.3 per cent and the output per direct operator rose annually by 7 per cent to 1590 shirts per year.

Profitability is relatively low for an industry with the level of risk associated with the shirt business; the ratio of fixed interest capital to total capital employed is very different between independent and subsidiary companies.

3.1 Sources of information

To avoid duplication of effort, relatively little investigation has been carried out into activities of the industry for which a reliable and reasonably up-to-date source of information already exists. One authoritative source, to which reference will be made in this Chapter, is the recently published report No. 110 of the National Board for Prices and Incomes, entitled *Pay and conditions in the clothing manufacturing industries†*, which includes information on the shirt manufacturing sector for Great Britain; data for Northern Ireland was obtained from the Ministry of Health and Social Security, through the Department of Employment and Productivity. In the absence of readily available information, the distribution of establishments by size (in terms of the number of employees per establishment) has been taken to be similar to that in Great Britain.

A future basic source of information, both on the shirt industry as a whole and on individual organisations, will be the data which companies now have to file with the Registrar of Companies under the 1967 Finance Act. The data will be particularly valuable when sufficient time has elapsed for filing to be complete, and information on several years' trading by a company will enable its performance in a particular year to be seen in perspective. This chapter refers to certain financial aspects revealed by an examination of the figures so far filed, but no extrapolation to form a complete picture of the whole industry is yet practicable, as a number of companies in the industry have not yet filed the relevant data.

3.2 Size and structure

According to the NBPI report and the DEP data, the UK shirt industry at the end of 1968 comprised some 750 separate manufacturing establishments, employing almost 37,000 people. The shirt manufacturers employed about 8.8 per cent of the total labour force in the home clothing industry and produced about 7.1 per cent of the total clothing turnover in value. They employed a higher proportion of female labour than all but two other sectors (dressmaking and corsetry), and on average were

---

*This figure excludes managers and supervisors and corresponds to the Wages Council's coverage of labour. The term 'direct operator' where used refers to personnel who contribute directly to the conversion of fabric into a shirt. Examiners and other ancillary staff are excluded. In this study 'direct operators' are assumed to be 95 per cent of all employees as defined here.

†*Pay and conditions in the clothing manufacturing industries*, HMSO Cmnd 4002, 6s 6d

organised in slightly larger operating units than most of the other sectors. The comparative figures for the sectors are given in Table 3.1 for Great Britain, which is broadly representative of the United Kingdom as a whole.

A more detailed analysis of the present structure of the industry can be obtained from the information given in Figure 3.1 which is a modified version of NBPI data.

Table 3.1 Clothing industry employment in Great Britain

Clothing sector *	Total employment (000s)	% Female	Average size of establishment (employees)
Shirts	29	92	48
Ready made	169	83	65
Dressmaking (total)	137	93	40
Wholesale mantle	61	72	35
Corsetry	23	93	104
Retail bespoke (total)	10	52	5
Rubber proofed	2.9	79	45

*All sectors by Wages Council definitions except dressmaking and retail bespoke.

To compare the pattern of establishment size with that for output by establishment size it is necessary to consider the variations in manpower productivity in terms of number of shirts produced per employee per year across the industry. Although no detailed statistics are available, it is evident that the larger production units in general concentrate on longer runs of similar articles, and have a rather higher manpower productivity than the smaller establishments. From an examination of data from a number of shirt producing units in the UK and abroad received during the course of the study, the pattern of productivity given in Table 3.2 has emerged; in this table the productivity of establishments of different sizes is shown in relation to that existing in an establishment with more than 333 employees. The relative productivity ratios presented in Table 3.2 have been used in preparing Figure 3.2.

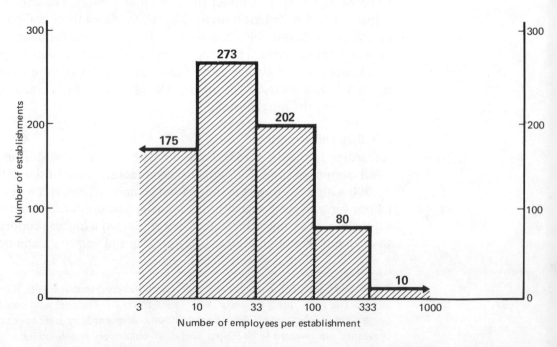

FIGURE 3.1 – NUMBER OF PRODUCTION UNITS BY ESTABLISHMENT SIZE IN 1968

14

Table 3.2 Pattern of average manpower productivity

Establishment size (total employment)	Ratios of manpower productivity
1–9	0.4
10–32	0.6
33–99	0.8
100–333	0.9
333 upwards	1.0

The data shown in Figure 3.2 emphasises the higher unit production achieved by the much larger establishments, although all but the smallest made a significant contribution to total industry output in 1968.

From the point of view of companies in the industry, the structural pattern is of particular importance. Although the currently limited availability of information filed at Companies House prevents a comprehensive survey from being carried out, certain observations on the industry's structure can be made.

It is estimated that the UK shirt industry comprised about 250 separate companies in 1968, the largest number of manufacturing units operated by a single shirt manufacturing company being six. A number of the companies are themselves linked in groups, but even the largest group, the shirt interests of the Viyella organisation, supplied no more than 12 per cent of the total home market by value in 1968. Other large multi-sector textile groups, such as Courtaulds and English Calico, have sizeable shirt manufacturing interests, while several groups, such as J H Buckingham and William Pickles, are involved in other sectors of the clothing trade as well as being actively concerned in the shirt business; some 13 per cent by value of home shirt production is accounted for by these multi-company groups. In addition, to these groups there is the family of companies who concentrate on supplying Marks and Spencer, who between them account for upwards of 15 per cent of the total market by value, although the shirt manufacturing companies involved are not linked in any way apart from their common allegiance to a single customer.

The remainder of the home output of shirts, amounting to 60 per cent by value, is supplied by mainly independent companies which vary widely in size and character and cover all sectors of the home market.

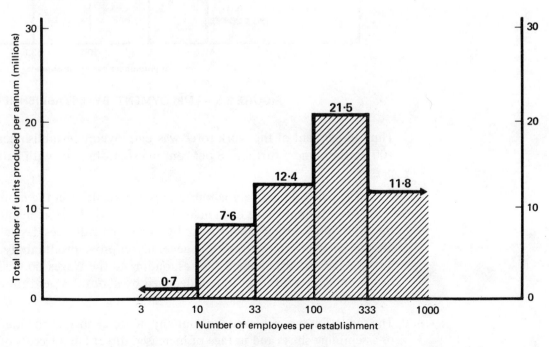

FIGURE 3.2 – OUTPUT BY ESTABLISHMENT SIZE IN 1968

15

The industry, then, presents a highly fragmented appearance. It appears that even the grouped companies make little use of the potential benefits of operating as a group, apart from their readier access to finance from the parent organisation.

3.3 Employment
Although the shirt manufacturing sector is only the fourth largest employer of labour in the clothing industry as a whole (Table 3.1), its manpower is one of its most valuable resources at present, and will continue to be so for many years to come.

The number of workers employed in 1968, as stated above (3.2), was 37,000, of whom 92 per cent were women; if managers and supervisors are included, the ratio of female to male employees falls to around 90 per cent.

The distribution of employees of all types by size of establishment is given in Figure 3.3 again based on data from the NBPI report and the DEP relating to the position at the end of 1968

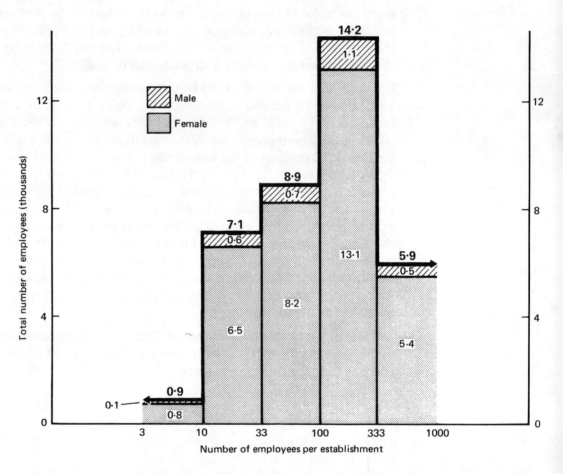

FIGURE 3.3 – EMPLOYMENT BY ESTABLISHMENT SIZE

Thus 46 per cent of the work force was employed in establishments with fewer than 100 persons, and a further 38 per cent in establishments with between 100 and 333 persons.

As in virtually all relatively labour-intensive industries in the more highly developed countries, attempts have been made in the past by the shirt manufacturers to improve the utilisation of their labour force by introducing devices designed to reduce operator fatigue, shorten training time and generally improve productivity. Figure 3.4 shows how the labour cost element (corresponding to the Wages Council's coverage of labour) of the industry's turnover in fact declined by about 7.3 per cent during the years 1960–68.

The reduction was achieved without any major change in the method of constructing or assembling shirts and in face of increased direct labour costs of between 51 per cent (female) and 61 per cent (male). This increase is in terms of current prices. Up to 1962,

16

the rising earnings were not compensated by an increase in productivity. From 1962 to 1965, however, the industry was enabled to reduce the direct labour content of its production by the increasing development by the machinery makers of devices, attachments and operating systems specifically designed to reduce labour content rather than improve the quality or performance of particular operations. There is less evidence of reduction after 1965, although it appeared from information gained from visits made during the study, to have continued in the USA and West Germany.

Over the eight-year period, the industry made a corresponding improvement in output per direct operator, as shown in Figure 3.5, which is based on the output figures given in Figure 2.1. As the average real value (at retail or manufacturers' selling price level) of the shirts produced at home has varied little over the past ten years (see Table 2.1) the output in value terms follows a very similar pattern.

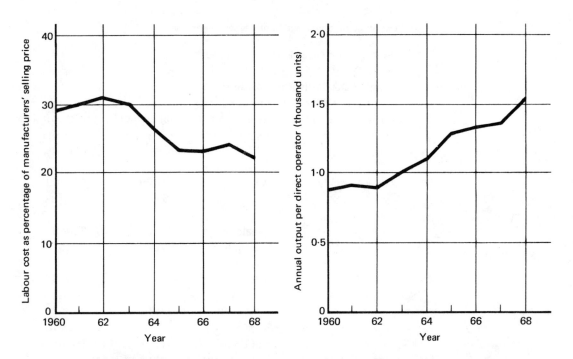

FIGURE 3.4 – LABOUR COST AS PERCENTAGE
OF MANUFACTURERS SELLING PRICE

FIGURE 3.5 – ANNUAL OUTPUT PER
DIRECT OPERATOR

In average number of units produced per direct operator, output rose from 920 shirts per year in 1960 to 1590 per year in 1968, an average rate of increase of about 7 per cent per year. This is equivalent to a rise from £1100 to about £1990 per year at manufacturers' selling prices in current value terms. However, the rise was at least partly due to the elimination of many of the smaller companies over the period, and not only to a labour productivity increase.

The apparently high increases in annual output for employees in 1965 and 1968 were due as much to the increased market demands which led to high levels of overtime being worked as to significant improvements in actual plant efficiency.

Although actual average earnings, as opposed to the basic recommended levels, vary widely between individual shirt producing companies, the general picture, as shown below, is one in which the shirt industry tends to pay rather less than clothing as a whole, both men's and women's average earnings being significantly lower than the average for all manufacturing industries. This is true for both male and female workers, and although there was an upward shift in women's earnings during 1969, marginally higher in shirts than in clothing as a whole, there is still a disparity in favour of other sections of the clothing trade, and of all manufacturing as a whole.

As no detailed statistics were drawn up during the study itself, these comments are based in the data given below.

Table 3.3 **The pattern of earnings**
From NBPI Report,* November 1968 (GB only)

Earnings in s d

		Shirts	*Clothing*
Average weekly	Male	411s 2d	419s 2d
	Female (full time)	218s 3d	229s 5d
Average hourly	Male	9s 8d	10s 0d
	Female (full time)	5s 7d	5s 11d

Definition of 'Shirts' and 'Clothing' by Wages Council.

*HMSO, Cmnd 4002, 6s 6d

From NEDO Statistical Bulletin (UK)
Earnings in s d for October 1968.
Figures in brackets give rise in earnings during 12 months to October 1969.

		Shirts	*Clothing*	*All manufacturing*
Average weekly	Male	381s 0d (+5.5)	407s 0d (+5.7)	472s 0d (+8.5)
	Female (full time)	204s 0d (+5.5)	220s 0d (+4.5)	226s 0d (+7.1)
Average hourly	Male	–	9s 6d (+8.8)	10s 4d (+8.5)
	Female (full time)	–	5s 10d (+6.0)	5s 11d (+8.2)

Definitions of sectors, within Standard Industrial Classification, as below:
Shirts—Minimum list heading (MLH) 444
Clothing—MLHs 441–6 and 449
All Manufacturing—Orders III–XIX
DEP figures quoted.

3.4 Financial position

Figure 3.6 shows the pattern of profitability in 1968 of the 64 companies which have filed relevant information and are now in business, measured as pre-tax profits against net assets employed; as far as possible, an allowance of assets and profit has been made for any non-shirt manufacturing activities after discussion with the companies concerned.

This financial data is of course based on book values of assets, and must therefore be regarded with a measure of caution. There is, however, no reason to suppose that general comparisons between companies of different sizes will be invalidated, even though absolute values of profitability for individual companies may not be directly comparable.

With few exceptions, the pattern of profitability appears to be distinctly related to the level of net assets employed. Of the companies with net assets employed of over £500,000 who have filed returns – they include most of the large UK shirt manufacturers – the great majority fall within a clear band of 5 per cent to 30 per cent per year profitability: only one of the thirteen large companies which filed returns falls outside this band, with a return of about 3 per cent of net assets. As explained in Appendix D, a return of 20 per cent per year is at present taken as a minimum acceptable for an

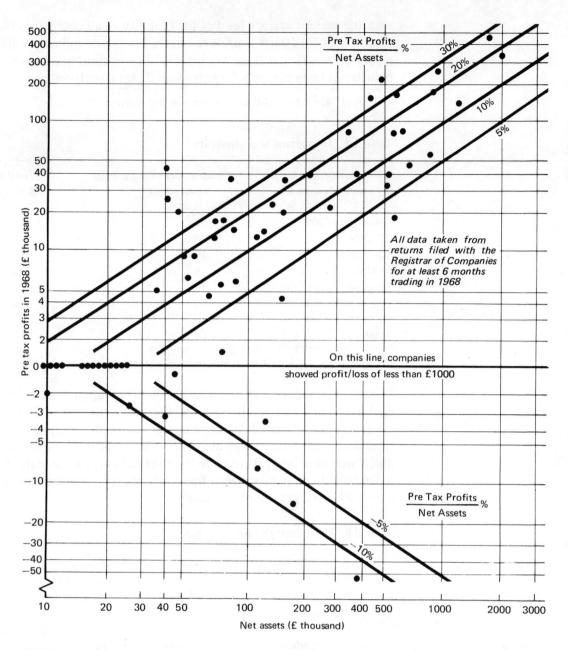

FIGURE 3.6 – THE PROFITABILITY OF A SAMPLE OF UK SHIRT MANUFACTURERS

industry with the level of risk associated with the shirt business, as this is no greater than the rate of return now set as a target for many nationalised concerns. However only a small proportion of the larger companies appear to have reached this level in what was regarded by the shirt industry as a relatively good trading year.

A quite different pattern of profitability emerges for the middle size band of companies, with net assets employed of between £500,000 and £50,000. Here there is a much wider range of performance, and, while seven of the twenty-eight companies which filed returns achieved the 20 per cent return referred to above, no fewer than five failed to make any profit at all in 1968. The average return is slightly over 15 per cent, with no particular trend as to size within the band.

The smaller companies recorded, with net assets employed of less than £50,000, are probably the least representative of their section of the industry, since a large number have not filed returns. Nevertheless, there is a marked drop in the apparent profitability when they are compared with the larger companies.

Of the 23 returns, 18 show a negligible profit or loss for 1968, three show a profitability of up to 30 per cent, and three a profitability of over 30 per cent per year.

The overall tendency appears to be for the large companies to be the least likely to make a loss or a very low profit (less than 5 per cent return on net assets); but for all sizes the present average level of profitability of all companies filing returns, except the most successful 20 per cent, is relatively low for an industry with this level of risk. It must be stressed that there are successful companies of all sizes at present; but the industry at large can only be judged on its total performance.

The profitability of the companies is summarised in Table 3.4

Table 3.4   The pattern of profitability

Pre-tax profit/loss % net assets employed	Number of companies covered	Total net assets involved £ million
Greater than 30%	7	1.1
20–30%	8	3.9
10–20%	16	6.0
5–10%	8	3.0
Less than 5% profit or loss	19	1.7
Loss of more than 5%	6	0.8
Total	64	16.5

Net assets are defined as total assets less current liabilities (not including bank loans).

In Table 3.5, the sources of capital of the 64 companies are analysed, exclusive of net creditors, and the ratio of fixed interest capital to total capital employed — ie the 'gearing' ratio — derived. It became clear during the compilation of the table that the capital sources of the companies who were subsidiary to a parent organisation, which might well have interests outside the shirt industry, were quite different to those of the independent companies; hence financial data for subsidiary and independent companies has been presented separately.

Table 3.5   The industry's sources of capital

	Total equity £ million			Total fixed interest capital £ million			Total capital £ million	Gearing ratio %
	Ordinary shares	Reserves	Minority interest	Preference shares	Long term loans	Overdraft and short term loans		
Independent companies	8.0	24.2	3.2	0.7	0.4	2.5	39.0	9.3
Subsidiary companies	2.3	4.2	–	0.1	0.7	3.3	10.6	38.8
Total	10.3	28.4	3.2	0.8	1.1	5.8	49.6	15.5

It is clear that, for the companies covered by the financial returns the subsidiaries operate at a much higher gearing than the independents, showing the greater degree to which they are prepared (or able) to make use of fixed interest rather than equity capital.

In considering this, two factors must be borne in mind: firstly the level of stocks held varies throughout the year, especially for companies producing for the fashion and thus seasonally dependent part of the market; and secondly the level of overdraft shown in the annual accounts also varies according to the financial year ending dates. Normally the overdraft shown in accounts for years ending between, say, 31 December and the end of April is rather lower than for years ending at, say, the end of August or September, due to the relatively large volume of sales made in the last quarter of a year.

However, a comparison between the respective gearings of companies with financial years ending in the first half of the year with those ending in the latter half showed only a slight difference; and in both cases, the ratio of the apparent gearing of independent to subsidiary companies was broadly maintained, indicating that, in this respect at least, the subsidiary companies were able to take advantage of their dependence on a parent group, regardless of the date on which their annual accounts ended.

Chapter 4 Distribution and promotion

The pattern of material and product flow is outside manufacturers' control, but they can choose their individual suppliers and marketing routes. Distribution channels vary widely; wholesalers' sales to retailers suffer marketing and price disadvantages by comparison with direct sales.

Among outlets chain stores and multiple outfitters are increasing their share of the trade at the expense of department stores and independents, although independents still hold about a third of the market. Direct sales from warehouses (excluding mail order) are a growing outlet for shirts.

The average annual rate of purchasing shirts is 4 per consumer in the UK, compared with around 6 in West Germany and 8 in the USA.

Advertising expenditure on branded shirts is low by the standards of other consumer goods, and only about half that of American branded shirt manufacturers.

4.1 Flow of materials and products

The flow of products within the shirt industry, from the raw material stage to sale to the consumer, is shown in Figure 4.1. The data, which has been rounded to the nearest

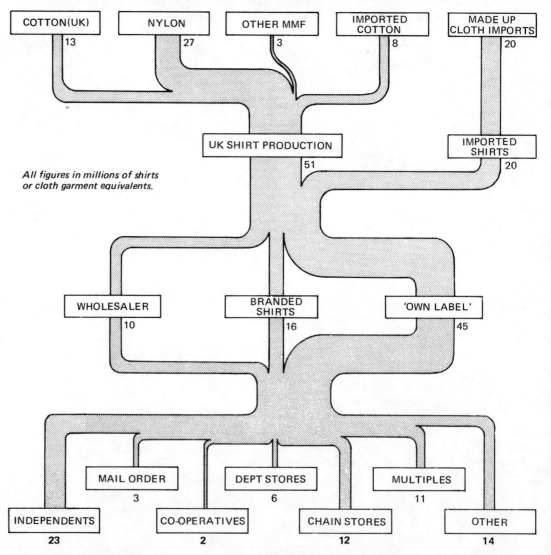

All figures in millions of shirts or cloth garment equivalents.

FIGURE 4.1 – FLOW OF MATERIALS AND PRODUCTS IN 1969

million units, is drawn from a number of sources, including ICI Fibres, HM Customs and Excise, and estimates obtained from the industry; the outlet types are defined in Appendix A.

The pattern of material and product flow illustrated is largely outside the control of the shirt manufacturers, but they are at liberty to choose their individual material suppliers and individual marketing route – for example, independent retailer, mail order house or variety chain.

4.2 Distribution channels

Distribution channels of shirts from manufacturers to consumers vary considerably. Multiple retailers, particularly the larger ones, tend to buy the majority of their supplies as 'own-label' merchandise direct from the manufacturer, and take delivery at either their individual stores or a central warehouse.

Branded manufacturers sell through their sales forces to independent retailers and to multiples stocking branded shirts, and likewise deliver to individual stores or the central warehouses of large organisations; in the latter case, reduced distribution costs allow quantity discounts to be demanded and granted. Wholesalers often distribute their own brands of shirt; they cover the independent retailers, too, but in the main supply those who are not considered economic by the larger manufacturer. In practice, they tend to handle the cheaper shirts which they sell under their own label. They cannot, however, promote their own brands as energetically as the branded manufacturers with their own sales forces, since they carry many menswear items and must spread their effort accordingly.

Table 4.1 compares typical costs of direct distribution of branded shirts and of similar shirts sold through wholesalers.

In this table, representative costs incurred by a large branded shirt manufacturer in performing necessary operations from the completion of actual production to delivery to a customer are compared with typical wholesalers' charges; it is clear that an additional cost of some 7d per shirt – some 2½ per cent of the total price to the retailer – results from the use of a wholesaler at the present levels of wholesale mark-up. It is thus likely that, in the future, the wholesalers' position will come under greater pressure as individual manufacturers become more aggressive in their marketing policies unless they can cut their discount to perhaps 15 per cent so as to offer retailers a real price advantage.

Table 4.1 Costs of distribution

	Pence per shirt Direct to outlet	Through wholesaler
Assumed production cost (as of medium quality shirt)	240	240
Stockholding (10% of average stocks)	5	–
Sale office	13	1
Field sales costs	18	,6
Transport and warehouse	23	3
Total manufacturers' price	299	250
Plus 22½% (wholesale only)	–	56
Total	299	306

The adoption of a cash-and-carry system might give wholesalers the opportunity to cut costs. This system has met with success in the food industry, where some years ago wholesalers faced similar problems: the larger wholesalers formed voluntary chains whereby each became the central buying and distribution point for a group of retailers, which are themselves not financially linked, and cash-and-carry methods were introduced to serve the many remaining small retailers. A difficulty could, however, be that quantity discounts being less highly developed in menswear than in the grocery trade, the system might be slower in achieving general acceptance.

4.3 Retail outlets

The percentage sales by each type of outlet in 1967 and 1969, based on ICI Fibres data, are shown in Table 4.2

Table 4.2 Sales of shirts by type of outlet 1967 and 1969

Type of outlet	Percentage by volume 1967	1969
Chain Stores	16	17
Multiples { outfitters	11	13
Multiples { tailors	2	3
Department stores	10	8
Independents { outfitters	36	30
Independents { tailors	2	3
Co-operative societies	6	3
Mail order	4	4
Market stalls	4	4
Others	9	15

The main trend in distribution at present is for the chain stores and the multiple outfitters to increase their share of the trade at the expense of the department stores and independent outfitters. This has important implications for the manufacturers of advertised brands; it means that their best outlets are shrinking, as the chains and multiples tend to sell the leading own-label brands. Other trends are the movement of certain multiple tailors into complete outfitting and an increase in the proportion of shirts sold through wholesale warehouses, direct to the public at a discount. The latter are becoming a major outlet for imported shirts, and accounted for a significant part of the 'other' category in 1969.

4.4 Advertising and promotion

In comparison with many other consumer markets, advertising expenditure on shirts is relatively low. Advertising only occurs in a limited part of the branded shirt trade, and even those UK shirt manufacturers who do advertise spend no more than about 50 per cent of the advertising budgets of their counterparts in the USA and West Germany. Recent UK advertising expenditure levels are given in Table 4.3

This expenditure is at about the rate of 3 per cent of the turnover of the shirt companies' advertising, which compares with about 6 per cent spent by the large American and West German branded manufacturers consulted during visits abroad; and total spending on advertising by the UK industry amounts to no more than ½ per cent of the total retail turnover of all shirts. These percentages would seem to be inadequate if manufacturers' brands are really to flourish. A feature of large consumer markets

Table 4.3 Advertising expenditure by major shirt brands

Shirt brand	1966 £	1967 £	1968 £
Banner	37,466	11,461	18,427
Double Two and Top Twenty	102,800	102,500	164,000
Peter England	46,760	64,190	55,483
Rocola	10,209	33,310	41,412
Van Heusen	70,320	72,882	71,145
Viyella	16,888	24,246	11,973
Rael Brook	88,619	66,439	77,936
Tootal	90	11,034	70
Mr Harry			47,685
Rochester	8,144	689	1,911
Mentor	7,427	111	8,377
Tern	56,929	58,924	50,953
Tricopress		5,295	66,263
Melka	8,066	303	505
TOTAL	£453,718	£451,384	£616,140

Source: Legion Publishing Company

where manufacturers do little advertising is that, since the task of influencing the consumer is left to the retailer, retailers' brands tend to thrive; thus the manufacturers lose the initiative to the retailer and become manufacturing suppliers only.

Branded manufacturers, whether they advertise or not, also spend further sums, probably amounting to ½ per cent or less of turnover, on point-of-sale material such as display stands, show cards, etc.

A comment on the creative content of shirt advertisements would be inappropriate here because of the high degree of subjectivity involved. But it can be stated factually that few shirt companies give to the formulation of their advertising copy the attention it receives in most consumer goods companies, or use consumer research to assist them in devising the most suitable copy. This is in marked contrast to the American shirt industry where all the largest firms are aware that as their market changes their advertising approach must change too, and each is able to define precisely what it is trying to put over in its advertising.

In the US the average rate of purchasing shirts, by the individual consumer, is over 8 per year, and in West Germany 6 per year, compared with 4 per year in the UK. This may well be at least partly the result of their larger advertising budgets, greater appreciation of consumers' requirements, and deeper knowledge of advertising techniques.

Chapter 5   Production costs in the United Kingdom

In establishing costs, three representative types of shirt – the commodity, the medium-quality and the specialist shirt – are chosen for investigation, and certain price levels are assumed for materials, manpower and plant. On this basis existing factories with an annual production of 600,000 commodity or 300,000 medium-quality shirts are found to be vulnerable to competition from newly built factories in the same location with a production 3–4 times greater; this is even after allowing for the full cost of the capital associated with the new plant and buildings. Transfer of production on the same scale to a Northern Ireland development area, where manpower and capital costs are less, can be justified for the larger plants, employing more than about 250 direct operators.

5.1 Establishing the costs

In examining manufacturing and marketing costs in the UK and overseas three distinct types of shirt have been selected as representative of the range of shirts available to the UK market. The selection was made after a number of visits and discussions with manufacturers and customers at home and abroad. The three types are: the commodity shirt, the medium-quality shirt, and the specialist shirt. The commodity shirt is simple in design and cheap to produce in long runs, and sells on price alone; typical of many imported shirts, it is often distributed to the consumer through mass distribution centres such as supermarkets and mail order channels. The medium-quality shirt is made of better material than the commodity shirt and is designed to last longer. Design and production do not allow fancy variations in its style, and it sells on a basis of value for money rather than cheapness. It is typical of the widely distributed branded shirts. The specialist shirt comes in a wide variety of styles and designs, and its production costs allow for minute attention to detail and quality. Price is not of major importance to the consumer who is more interested in its style and individuality. Its distribution is limited, and manufacturing costs are relatively unimportant, as exclusiveness has its own advantages in creating the right image and market for the class of product. Technical specifications of the three types of shirt are given in Appendix B, page 78.

Methods of manufacturing the three representative shirts are assumed to be those of a well run, modern unit, and production rates those attainable by an efficient management – rates decided upon after visits to companies manufacturing each type of shirt at home and abroad. UK costs given are basically those for non-development areas, such as apply in the South-East, and a comparison with production costs in Northern Ireland is added at the end of this chapter (5.4). (Costs relate to mid 1969).

5.2 Basic information

Before presenting production costs it may be helpful to give some basic information on the main items in the costing – cloth, other materials, manpower and plant.

Cloth

The representative costings are based on the two fabrics used or present in over 90 per cent of shirt making.

Warp knitted fabric at present largely continuous filament nylon, ranges from very lightweight, at 6.4 yd per lb, to heavier fabric, at 4.6 yd per lb. The former is sold to the trade as unbranded nylon, and even knitted sometimes on in-house secondhand warp knitting machinery. Its use is limited to commodity shirts. Medium-quality shirts use branded nylon at between 5.3 and 4.9 yd per lb, and specialist shirts use branded nylon at around 4.6 yd per lb. The price of nylon fabric is at present fairly 'soft', and quantity discounts range up to 7½ per cent below nominal prices, which, for plain colours and typical quantities of 10,000 yd, are here assumed to be:

Type of nylon	Price per sq yd
Unbranded, 6.4 yd per lb	24d
Branded, 5.3 yd per lb	39.5d
Branded, 4.6 yd per lb	57d

Woven shirting fabrics are mostly of two types at present: cotton and polyester/cotton. Cottons range from cheap imported Hong Kong fabric to the finest Sea Island material. In this report, a price of 38½d per sq yd is assumed for the cheapest home-produced cotton fabric, the equivalent from Hong Kong landing at 12–15 per cent less; Sea Island cottons range up to 95d or 100d per yd for two-fold yarn. A standard polyester/cotton fabric, home-produced, for use in a medium-quality shirt costs 58½d per lin yd 42 in width, equivalent fabric from Hong Kong costing about 25 per cent less in the UK. Usual order sizes for woven fabrics are from 50,000 to 100,000 yd in white and about 50,000 yd in a colour but small orders down to 5,000 yd are placed by small companies; quantity discounts are again up to about 7½ per cent.

Other materials
Buttons, bones, fusible patches, linings and thread vary enormously in cost according to the quality of the shirt. Buttons for example range from 8½d to 10s per gross. Linings rise from 2s 6d to 10s per yd, and the quantity per shirt increases with the quality. Fusibles range from 2s 6d to 5s per yd.

Manpower
Labour costs comprise gross pay, plus the employer's contribution to holidays, national insurance and graduated pensions. They are calculated for the South-East and Midlands – that is, the non-development areas. In development areas earnings are up to 10 per cent less, so that in the special case where the Regional Employment Premium is allowed, total labour costs drop to 85 per cent of the rate assumed for the South-East. These typical earnings and total annual cost of different categories of personnel, are set out in Table 5.1, having been derived from data supplied by a number of shirt producers in the UK and discussed with Union representatives.

Attainable productivity rates for a 40-hour week are assumed for the purposes of this investigation to be 120 commodity shirts, 80 medium-quality shirts or 50 specialist shirts per operator, the term 'operator' covering personnel who contribute directly to the conversion of fabric into a shirt, from fabric store to pressing and folding, but excluding examiners, supervisors, foremen and ancillary staff. These rates are based on rates currently being obtained by the most efficient firms in the UK and Western Europe. It must be noted that they are over twice the industry average.

Plant buildings and working capital
Three sizes of factory, employing respectively 50, 150 and 450 operators (as defined above) have been costed. Their capital cost, based on the square footage, including offices, toilets, canteen (in the two larger sizes only) and site amenities, is:

No. of operators	Productive area	Capital cost
50	8,500	£48,000
150	21,000	£120,000
450	58,500	£290,000

Precise figures for the cost of land cannot be given, since some companies build on their existing sites, for others the cost of new land is considerable, and for others again the cost is reduced or covered by the sale of an existing site.

The investment in plant needed to give the attainable productivities given above is indicated in Figure 5.1, which shows the economies of scale obtainable in shirt producing equipment, as broken down between machines, finishing equipment, cutting room and services.

Table 5.1 Average representative costs of manpower

Overhead staff		Earnings £	Total annual cost £
Manager	m	2,050 pa	2,264
Secretary	f	14.0 pw	864
Chief Mechanic	m	26.5	1,588
Mechanic	m	24.0	1,453
Assistant mechanic	m	12.0	804
Canteen Manager	f	13.5	815
Canteen assistant	f	8.5	543
Cleaner	f	7.5	492
Clerical	f	15.0	897
Production personnel			
Foreman	m	26.0	£1,560
Senior supervisor	f	19.0	1,114
Examination supervisor	f	15.0	894
Examiner	f	10.5	651
Stock cutter	m	16.0	1,021
Stock cutter	f	10.5	652
Senior bandknife cutter	m	25.0	1,506
Junior bandknife cutter	m	16.0	1,021
Machinist	f	12.0	787
Presser/folder	f	10.0	625

In the costings, capital costs are recovered by adding a charge for capital to the conversion cost (as explained in Definitions and Assumptions, page xvii) to give the 'comprehensive conversion cost'. The charge in a development area is 74.5 per cent of the charge in the non-development areas, and in Northern Ireland even lower at 59.3 per cent, due to the rebates allowed on plant and machinery (Appendix E).

Total working capital is assumed to be one-quarter of the annual conversion cost, and the effective annual charge for this capital in the UK is taken as 4.2 per cent of conversion costs, as derived in Appendix E.

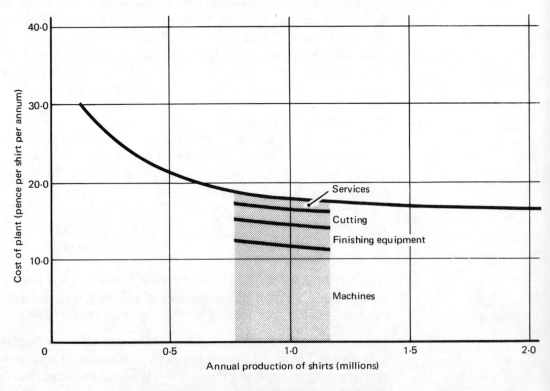

FIGURE 5.1 – INVESTMENT IN PLANT

5.3 Total production costs

Figure 5.2 shows the costs of manufacturing commodity shirts at various production rates. The economies of scale, whose effects are indicated, mean that any existing factory producing fewer than some 600,000 shirts a year is vulnerable to competition from a newly built factory, with full capital charges to pay off, producing 2 million shirts a year, assuming that both factories take full advantage of their size in utilising plant and in their method of operation. The effect is illustrated in Figure 5.2 at point A. The comparison assumes that production is carried out in the same location; comparison with overseas competition is made in Chapter 6.

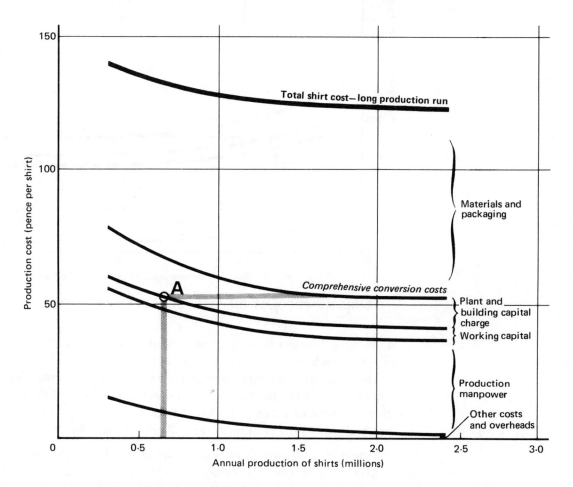

FIGURE 5.2 – PRODUCTION COSTS OF NYLON COMMODITY SHIRT

The future costs of commodity shirt manufacturing will tend to lead to larger production units. Fabric purchase, the biggest element in the production cost, can be organised more economically for one large unit. Shift working, on the other hand, does not as a rule bring any advantages, the existing shift allowances more than matching the potential saving in fixed costs in the present state of machinery development.

The costs of producing polyester/cotton medium-quality shirts, both in long production runs and in short runs allowing for changes of style about once every five weeks, are shown in Figure 5.3. Here, the economies of scale suggest that an existing factory turning out less than about 300,000 shirts a year, as shown by point B in Figure 5.3, is vulnerable to competition from a new factory of 1.3 million shirts a year capacity or more, both units being operated to the same standards in the same location. For this type of shirt, as for the commodity shirt, is is assumed that no technological advance will dramatically change the most efficient shirt manufacturing methods in the next five years; when advances do come, they are likely to increase the pressure to build larger production units.

It will be noticed that materials and packaging for a medium-quality shirt form a larger proportion of the total cost than for the commodity shirt. As with the latter, manpower

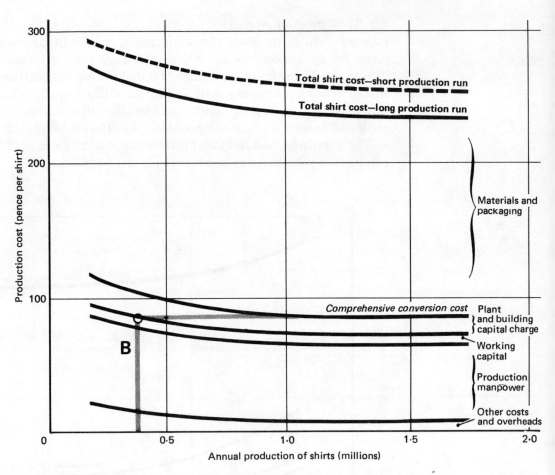

FIGURE 5.3—PRODUCTION COSTS OF POLYESTER/COTTON MEDIUM QUALITY SHIRT

is the second largest item, and, again, shift working in not economically justifiable with the machinery currently available. Figure 5.3 also illustrates the effect of short runs of production of less than five weeks — an increase in costs of up to 12½ per cent over long-run production of five-week runs of constant style. If the recommendations made in Chapter 10 for more frequent changes of fabric and style are accepted, then the cost to the manufacturer will be increased by this order.

The costs of producing specialist shirts are not shown graphically, since they are of less significance and will vary widely with different garments. The main items for a small manufacturer of specialist shirts are typically as shown in Table 5.2. The economies of scale being uncertain, the size of production unit may well continue to be small, and there will be little pressure for growth on production grounds alone. The proportion of labour cost to total comprehensive conversion cost is about the same as for medium-quality shirts: the better quality of fabric is matched by increased work content and supervision.

Labour costs in the shirt industry are likely to rise in real terms as a result of future legislation for equal pay for women. An increase of 20 per cent in real terms in

Table 5.2 Production costs of specialist shirts

Fabric-Sea Island cotton, two-fold	234d per shirt
Linings, buttons, bones and thread	28
Packaging materials	20
Consumables, maintenance energy and services	11
Production manpower	107
Overhead staff	20
Working capital	17
Plant and buildings	25
Total cost per shirt	462d

women's wages, for example, would add about 13 per cent to the labour cost of a shirt (8d to the cost of a polyester/cotton shirt), or less than 4 per cent to the total shirt costs. Some estimates of the likely increase in labour costs put it at twice this level, but even this would produce only an increase of less than 8 per cent in the total manufacturing cost, extended over a period from the present time until the complete establishment of equal pay.

5.4 Development area costs

It has been pointed out above (5.2) that development areas offer lower manpower costs and capital charges than non-development areas. Comparative costs of medium-quality shirts for production units of three sizes in both types of area are shown diagrammatically in Figure 5.4. It will be seen that transferring production on the same scale to Northern Ireland can be justified for the largest plants, as the total production costs after transfer are less than the operating costs (material and manufacturing) in UK non-development areas. As the scale of production decreases, transfer to Northern Ireland becomes less attractive.

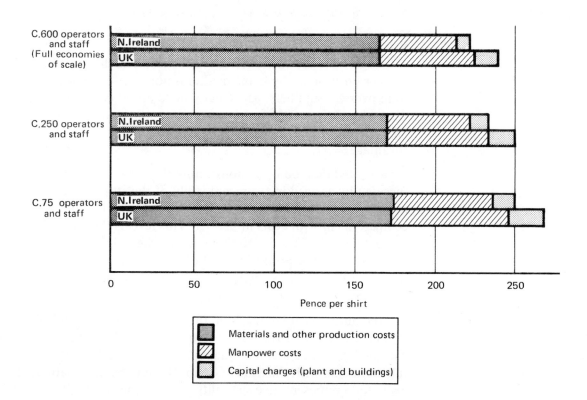

FIGURE 5.4—COMPARISON OF PRODUCTION COSTS IN THE UK AND N. IRELAND

Chapter 6 International cost comparison

Production costs of 3 selected shirts in 7 representative countries are compared by means of indices which establish a ratio for each individual item to its cost in the UK. Costs peculiar to imported shirts are added to make a fair comparison between their landed-at-port costs and the production costs of UK made shirts. In the UK, in commodity shirts, Portugal at present has economic advantages in nylon, Hong Kong in cotton, and Northern Ireland (using Hong Kong fabric) in polyester/cotton medium-quality shirts. The imposition of tariffs on Commonwealth cotton goods in 1972 and the UK's entry into the EEC, if it takes place, will alter the relative positions of the 7 countries, by a small amount. An analysis of competition in overseas markets shows that entry into the EEC would improve the UK's position in EEC as opposed to EFTA.

6.1 Evaluation of international performance

Although there are cost differences between UK shirt manufacturers, the main threat to their position in the home market is not inter-company competition but competition from overseas suppliers, particularly in commodity shirts which sell on price alone. Wage rates vary greatly from country to country and, shirt manufacturing being a highly labour-intensive industry, the low labour cost countries have a marked advantage.

An accepted method of demonstrating the level of international competition, successfully applied in the recent study of the strategic future of the wool textile industry, is to evaluate the costs of production in the different producer countries and compare them with costs in the UK. This reveals the strengths and weaknesses of competing manufacturers in the home market, vis-à-vis imports, and suggests overseas markets where UK producers might have an advantage in cost terms; the effect on their position of future changes in labour costs, tariffs or membership of trading communities can also be estimated.

For the purposes of comparison, the production of three different types of shirt in seven different countries has been investigated. Two commodity shirts, of nylon and cotton cloth, and a medium-quality shirt of polyester/cotton have been selected, after full discussion with the Study Group. No detailed international comparisons have been made for a representative speciality shirt, as the competitiveness of such garments cannot be assessed in cost terms alone. The three shirts are:

a commodity shirt in unbranded nylon fabric at 6.4 yd per lb
(27 sq yd per dozen shirts)

a commodity shirt in minimum iron finish cotton at 4.45 oz per sq yd
(27 sq yd per dozen shirts)

a medium quality shirt in 67/33 polyester/cotton at 3.6 oz per sq yd
(29 sq yd per dozen shirts)

Production is assumed to take place in a modern, well run factory, employing 200/250 personnel in each case — sufficiently large to allow reasonable economies of scale, even in manufacturing the commodity shirt, and the cost data derived in Chapter 5 has been used as a basis for UK production.

The seven producer countries, selected either for their current importance in the UK market, their possible future importance there, or their representative position as low-wage cost competitors, are the UK, Eire, Portugal, West Germany, Italy, USA and Hong Kong. Regarding the last criterion, Portugal and Hong Kong not only are current low-wage competitors themselves but represent the possible competition of other low-wage producers in the future, such as Malta, Tanzania, Brazil and Nigeria;

Portugal's competitiveness, for example, may well decline if its present rate of increase in wage rates of 8 per cent per year continues.

6.2 Basic costs at home and abroad

Table 6.1 gives indices which have been compiled to compare the various production costs in the selected countries. Some costs, like packaging, consumables and machinery, are not included in the table; although no comprehensive investigation has been carried out into the relative costs of these items in the various countries, it is believed that the majority vary little from one country to another.

Table 6.1 International cost indices

Country	Nylon	Polyester/ cotton	Cotton	Total wage cost	Total salaries costs	Linings	Electricity	Buildings	Central recovery on plant	Capital recovery on buildings	Working capital factor
United Kingdom	100	100	100	100	100	100	100	100	100	100	1.042
West Germany	85	99	–	143	167	100	130	120	102.9	123.5	1.037
Italy	–	99	–	109	156	100	109	100	113.2	113.2	1.045
Portugal	85	105	96	31	53	103	143	60	97.9	58.7	1.035
USA	–	86	–	259	214	100	63	100	123.9	123.9	1.050
Hong Kong	–	63	83	35	46	77	108	60	88.1	52.9	1.029
Eire	95	–	–	72	100	100	82	100	91.8	91.8	1.028

The indices reproduced in Table 6.1 have been derived as follows:

Cloth
The costs of cloth are given as indices of UK costs when woven in the country shown. The cloth imported from Hong Kong, particularly by the UK and Eire, is calculated as its landed cost to illustrate the effects of tariffs.

The UK costs are assumed to be as follows:

warp knit unbranded nylon at 6.4 yd per lb, pale shades: 23.8d per sq yd for large orders.

minimum iron white cotton at 4.45 oz per sq yd: UK produced, 38.5d per sq yd; landed in UK from Hong Kong at 33.8d per sq yd.

polyester/cotton, 67/33 mixture, permanent press finish, white, 3.6 oz per sq yd, 90 x 82 weave, 42 inch width: UK produced 58d per linear yd; landed in UK from Hong Kong, 38.0d per sq yd.

It can be seen that nylon is relatively cheap in West Germany and Portugal, and cheaper in Eire than the UK. Polyester/cotton from Hong Kong is particularly attractive in price to UK manufacturers. Hong Kong cotton is cheaper than the equivalent home-produced fabric, owing mainly to labour cost differentials, and some UK and Eire manufacturers find it advantageous at present to import both polyester/cotton and cotton fabrics from Hong Kong, although there have been problems with the control of quality.

Wages and salaries
Manpower costs include all additional costs, such as social security and holiday benefits, as well as wages and salaries. The potential output of employees, once trained, is

taken to be the same in all countries; this is in line with impressions gained from visits to the countries concerned and discussions with people with first hand knowledge of particular areas.

Changes in manpower costs are likely to affect international competitiveness more than any other factors, except perhaps variations in tariffs. Any rises in UK wage costs (5.2) will increase the attractiveness of the UK market to low-wage countries, but long-term changes in international competitiveness will only result if the rates of change in the respective earnings vary substantially over a period of time.

Linings

No attempt is made to show the effect of future tariffs on linings, and other ancillary materials, as their total cost is a relatively small part of the overall production cost and any effect is small indeed.

Electricity

Comparative costs are as obtained from the Electricity Council and from overseas government and operating board sources.

Buildings

The cost of building a shirt-manufacturing factory varies from country to country for two reasons: differences in the construction cost components, including wages, and differences in the type of building erected. Figures of comparative building costs supplied by the Ministry of Housing and Local Government incorporate both factors.

Capital recovery factors

These take into account the taxation of profits, investment grants and depreciation rates in each country. It is assumed that each expects a DCF rate of return of 10 per cent per year after taxation of profits, although in practice some countries may, on average, operate at a higher rate due to their current economic position, like West Germany, or to some other factor peculiar to themselves, like Hong Kong, where political uncertainty affects the rate.

The indices derived in Appendix E show that the UK enjoys lower capital charges than the EEC countries and the USA, although the advantage to the labour-intensive shirt industry in its present state of technology is relatively small. Portugal, Eire and Hong Kong have lower capital charges than the UK (apart from the development areas, Northern Ireland in particular).

6.3 Costs peculiar to imported shirts

For present purposes the ex-works cost of a UK manufactured shirt can be compared with the landed-at-port cost of an imported shirt, since distribution within the UK and sales costs from that moment can be considered as common to both. But, to obtain the landed cost, certain items peculiar to the imported shirt must be added to the costs — namely, sea transport, insurance, port dues, stockholding, an extra sales cost due to remote production, and tariffs.

The costs of transport, insurance and port dues, per shirt, compare as follows:

Commodity shirts, cotton, in bulk:

Hong Kong to London	0.9d
Lisbon to London	7.4d
Dublin to Liverpool	0.5d

Medium-quality shirts, polyester/cotton, individually boxed:

Hong Kong to London	16.7d
Lisbon to London	12.7d
Dublin to Liverpool	0.8d

Similar items on the North Atlantic run cost about the same as for Hong Kong to London.

34

Stocking costs, proportional to the total transit and port time, add a percentage to the cost of an imported shirt — typically 1.7 per cent for shirts from Hong Kong and 1.3 per cent for shirts from Portugal.

The cost of sales incurred by manufacture overseas is taken to be the cost of administration and expenses for the UK buyer. For commodity shirts in bulk from Eire the cost is 0.5d, from Portugal 2.3d and from Hong Kong 2.5d per shirt. Equivalent costs for medium-quality shirts are taken as twice these, on account of the greater variety and consequent selling effort per unit. The remaining cost incurred by imports is tariffs, as listed in Table 2.2.

6.4 Comparative production costs

To illustrate the method of calculating the costs of production overseas, the cost of manufacturing a nylon commodity shirt in Portugal is shown in detail in Table 6.2. For each item the UK cost of production is multiplied by the appropriate index for Portugal as given in Table 6.2.

Table 6.2 Production costs of nylon commodity shirt in Portugal and the UK

	Cost in UK— pence per shirt	Cost index for Portugal per cent	Cost in Portugal— pence per shirt
Nylon fabric	51.0	85	43.4
Linings	7.0	103	7.2
Other materials	3.1	100	3.1
Manpower—wages	38.5	31	11.9
—salaries	3.2	53	1.7
Electricity	0.7	143	1.0
Consumables	1.5	100	1.5
Services	2.8	100	2.8
Packaging	5.3	100	5.3
Total	113.1		77.9
x working capital factor	x 1.042		x 1.035
Total	117.9		80.6
Buildings	7.2	58.7	4.2
Plant	4.9	97.9	4.8
Total production cost	130.0		89.6

The results of the same calculation, applied to each type of shirt in each country, are represented diagrammatically in Figures 6.1, 6.2, and 6.3. The cloth, except where· shown to come from Hong Kong, is assumed to be locally produced. The UK figures are for a non-development area, the Northern Ireland figures for a special development area.

Among home production alternatives, Northern Ireland manufacture, using imported fabric, is most competitive with overseas manufacture on cost grounds, Hong Kong,

Portugal and Eire have the lowest production costs. The UK faces strong competition within EFTA from Portugal, but has lower production costs than the EEC countries.

6.5 Competition in the United Kingdom market

Finally, the production costs of the overseas countries can be summed together with the costs peculiar to imported shirts — transport, tariffs, etc. (as in 6.3 above) — to yield landed costs in the UK. The results, as they apply to the three representative

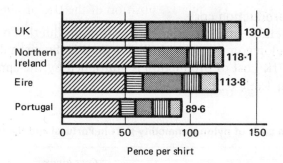

FIGURE 6.1 — INTERNATIONAL PRODUCTION COSTS OF NYLON COMMODITY SHIRT

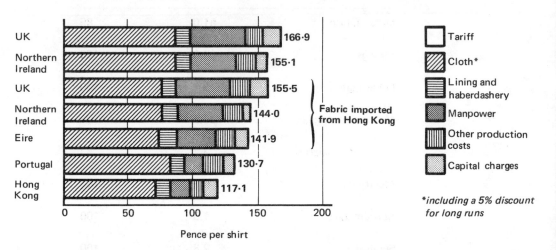

FIGURE 6.2 — INTERNATIONAL PRODUCTION COSTS OF COTTON COMMODITY SHIRT

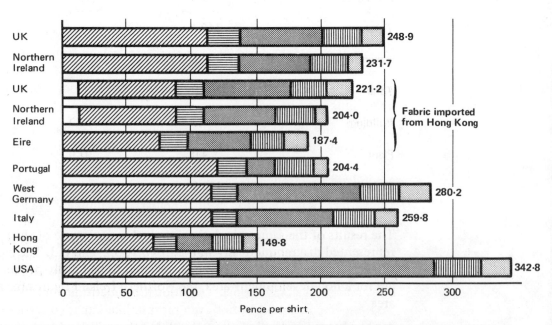

FIGURE 6.3 — INTERNATIONAL PRODUCTION COSTS OF POLYESTER/COTTON MEDIUM QUALITY SHIRT

36

shirts in present fiscal conditions, after the tariff changes of 1972, and in the event of UK joining EEC in, say, 1975, are shown in Table 6.3

In nylon commodity shirts, Portugal, enjoying the benefits of tariff-free trade within EFTA and of relatively cheap cloth, has the advantage; the cost of the Portuguese shirt is 78 per cent of the UK shirt, 85 per cent of the Northern Ireland shirt. There is little difference in cost between Eire and Northern Ireland.

In cotton, Hong Kong leads the field, the advantages of cheap cloth and low wages outweighing the disadvantage of distance. At present Hong Kong and Portugal compete on equal terms but in 1972 the imposition of import duty on Commonwealth cotton goods will favour Portugal. The relative position of the UK producer will also improve, particularly if located in Northern Ireland. After 1972, too, there will be no advantage in importing Hong Kong cotton fabrics, although Hong Kong polyester/cotton fabric will continue to show a cost advantage to the UK shirt manufacturer.

Table 6.3 Competition in the UK market

| | Rank, country of origin and comparative index | | | | | | |
	1st	2nd	3rd	4th	5th	6th	7th
Present							
Commodity nylon	Portugal 78	Eire 88	Northern Ireland 92	UK 100=130d			
Commodity Cotton	Hong Kong 78	Portugal 85	Eire* 86	Northern Ireland* 87	UK* 93	Northern Ireland 94	UK 100=167d
Medium quality polyester/cotton	Northern Ireland* 82	Hong Kong 84	UK* 89	Portugal 90	Eire* 92	Northern Ireland 94	UK 100=249d
1972 tariff change							
Commodity cotton	Portugal 85	Hong Kong 90	Northern Ireland 94	Northern Ireland* 94	UK* 100	UK 100=167d	Eire* 100
1975 if UK joins EEC							
Medium quality polyester/cotton	Hong Kong 80	Northern Ireland* 81	UK* 88	Eire* 89	Northern Ireland 93	UK 100=249d	Portugal 104

*Fabric imported from Hong Kong.

In polyester/cotton, shirts made in Northern Ireland from cloth imported from Hong Kong rank first followed by shirts made in Hong Kong. The UK producer ranks third in the home market, again using imported cloth from Hong Kong. The main effect of the UK joining the EEC would be to benefit Hong Kong at the expense of Portugal.

Eire generally enjoys a favourable position in the UK market, on account of its lower labour costs, its proximity, and the absence of import duties on fabric from the UK and on yarn, which are re-exported as shirts to the UK, again free of duty under the Anglo-Irish free trade agreement.

The pattern of competition in the UK market is unlikely to change significantly in the next few years, with the proviso that if the current rather more rapid rate of increase of wages in Hong Kong, Eire and Portugal is maintained, the competitiveness of the home shirt manufacturers will improve. In the case of the commodity shirts, it is possible that other developing countries, with wage levels below those of Hong Kong, Eire and Portugal, may provide additional competition, and thus effectively replace the current competition; it is, however, most unlikely that countries entering the shirt producing business will provide effective competition in the more fashion sensitive medium- and high-quality garments.

6.6 Competition in overseas markets

The same methods, as used for the UK market, are followed in evaluating the competition to UK shirts in overseas markets. The markets considered are West Germany, representing the EEC trading block, Sweden, representing EFTA countries, and the USA. The representative shirt in this case is the polyester/cotton medium-quality shirt.

Table 6.4 summarises the position in the three markets as it will be in 1972 and, assuming UK entry into the EEC, in 1975.

Entry into the EEC would improve the UK's position in West Germany, raising her from ninth to sixth place (using Hong Kong fabric, from fourth to third), ahead of the other EEC countries; and a Northern Ireland special development area would be even better placed. In the Swedish market, Portugal's prominent place as the cheapest European producer using its own cloth is due to low costs coupled with proximity to the market, which simplifies design problems. The UK's entry into the EEC would not improve its position, and relatively Portugal would gain an advantage in cost over the UK.

Table 6.4 Competition in overseas markets

Market	West Germany		Sweden		USA
Rank in market	1972–UK in EFTA	1975–UK in EEC	1972–UK in EFTA	1975–UK in EEC	1972
1st	Hong Kong 68	Hong Kong 80	Northern Ireland* 83	Hong Kong 73	Hong Kong 64
2nd	Eire* 76	Northern Ireland 81	Hong Kong 84	Eire* 75	Eire* 77
3rd	Northern Ireland* 82	UK* 88	Eire* 86	Portugal 78	Northern Ireland* 83
4th	UK* 89	Eire* 89	UK* 89	Northern Ireland* 82	Portugal 83
5th	Portugal 89	Northern Ireland 93	Portugal 90	UK* 89	UK* 89
6th	Italy 89	UK 100=251d	Northern Ireland 93	Northern Ireland 93	Northern Ireland 93
7th	Northern Ireland 93	Portugal 103	UK 100=251d	UK 100=288d	USA 98
8th	West Germany 96	Italy 104	Italy 119	Italy 104	UK 100=350d
9th	UK 100=293d	West Germany 112	West Germany 128	West Germany 112	Italy 104
10th					West Germany 111

*Fabric imported from Hong Kong

38

In the USA, unlike Sweden, home manufacturers have overcome local cost disadvantages mainly by vigorous marketing policies and diversification (10.6). Portugal's potentially strong position is again evident in this market, but the cost of a UK shirt landed in the USA is comparable with that of the home produced shirt.

Membership of EEC should not affect the UK's export of shirts adversely, and might indeed provide an incentive if a value added tax were to bring tax relief on exports within the terms of GATT. The position by 1975 may have changed if labour costs advance ahead of EEC rates. A rise of 20 per cent in real terms in wages for women, would as stated above (5.3), add some 4 per cent to the total cost of a shirt. But this, spread over five years, would not seriously affect UK's competitive position. Moreover, equal pay for women is already part of the EEC agreement, and the UK will not be alone in introducing it.

As in the home market, the position of the UK manufacturers is likely to improve in the future vis-à-vis those competitors whose labour costs are rising more rapidly than their own, and, as before (6.5), this will be particularly significant in the more fashion sensitive shirts, where there is unlikely to be additional competition in the near future from developing countries who are as yet not major shirt producers.

Part 2   The current environment

Chapter 7   The industry's strengths and weaknesses

The UK industry enjoys several advantages – some actual, some awaiting exploitation, over its competitors: proximity to the market, creativeness in design, resources of skilled manpower, low capital costs, good industrial relations, home knitted-cloth suppliers, a reputation for quality, and future membership of the EEC. Its main weaknesses are lack of bulk production facilities, of strong home woven-cloth suppliers and of home-based machinery suppliers.

7.1 The strengths of the industry

The UK shirt industry enjoys a number of advantages over virtually all its overseas competitors, simply by being the home-based industry in this country. Some of these have been realised in practice; others remain ready for exploitation when full advantage is taken of the potential growth in home demand for shirts.

Proximity

Proximity to his market brings the UK manufacturer many direct benefits: common language, currency, tax and credit arrangements, contract terms, and trading procedure with his customers; easy transport and communications; prompt and easily maintained quality control and colour matching between batches and sources of supply; and frequent and informal personal contact with both existing and prospective customers. Close contact with his customers is especially advantageous, in that he has knowledge of their existing problems and possible future demands, and can respond speedily to changes in their requirements. Mutual understanding and trust, strengthened by their common contacts in other fields, have every chance to grow.

Many of these benefits are, in general, beyond the reach of overseas manufacturers – as discussions with some half a dozen leading Portuguese manufacturers, in particular, confirm – and represent strengths on which the UK industry can capitalise.

Creativeness

Evidence was found during the course of the study to suggest that the creative strength of the UK shirt industry is fundamentally no greater than that of similar developed countries, such as West Germany, and in some respects, such as the supply of woven shirtings (7.2), it remains potential rather than actual. Nevertheless, a highly developed country like the UK has an inherent advantage over competitors in developing countries and in less highly developed countries with a different cultural background, which find it difficult to be creative in a foreign idiom, however efficient they may be in straightforward manufacturing. Countries like Hong Kong or even Portugal, adept at producing either low-cost articles of standard pattern in large quantities or relatively cheap imitations of other designs have, as yet, shown little signs of the necessary flair to set the pace in designing fashion products for the future. Efforts to improve management standards by injecting senior staff from more highly developed countries, as has been attempted in Portugal, appear to raise as many new problems in communication and labour relations as they solve.

Imports of commodity shirts have little or no value in stimulating the market to new thinking. On the other hand, limited imports of shirts of high quality and design from other highly-developed countries can serve as a stimulus to creativeness in fashion, design, colour and style.

Human resources

Although at first sight, this would appear as an area in which the UK is not well placed, sufficient personnel with a good background level of education are potentially available in the country, given the right training and conditions, to meet the needs of the shirt industry in the future. At the operator level, the lack of availability of cheap unskilled labour means that the level of technological advance must be geared to the better educated operators, so that optimum use can be made of the labour which is available. At other levels, staff and management are more readily available here than in any of the low labour cost shirt producers, provided that the shirt industry creates the opportunities to attract and hold the right people.

Investment

Although shirt manufacturing is not a highly capital intensive process, clearly a measure of investment is involved, especially in the setting up of new manufacturing units and in improving labour productivity. As shown in Appendix E, the special allowances granted in the development areas, and particularly those applicable in Northern Ireland, make the effective cost of capital investment as low as in any major potential competitor of the shirt industry. Thus, if a new investment to meet specific market demands is required, provided that labour is available, a favourable case can be put forward for it to be made in one or other of the development areas. These can indeed be more attractive than opportunities in overseas countries with lower labour costs, such as Portugal, where problems of management, procuring and training local labour, and maintaining quality and work standards, added to the uncertainties of international finance, would appear to make investment on a large scale by UK shirt manufacturing companies rather less attractive than it might seem from purely economic comparisons.

Industrial relations

Despite recent labour problems in certain sectors of the clothing industry, the shirt manufacturers enjoy a high level of co-operation between management and unions, and labour relations are better than in much of British industry. Owing to the preponderance of female labour, union membership has been limited in the past, and management-labour relations have been on a largely informal basis. The situation will, of necessity, change in the future, with equal pay bringing increased organisation of labour, and the likely growth in the average size of shirt manufacturing companies also leading to a more formalised pattern of industrial relations. Both management and unions will need to approach this new situation with care in order to make the most of the present good relations.

Technology

A further advantage over less developed countries is the UK's relatively high availability of technological education and facilities at the appropriate level, which gives it more expertise in the development of basic technology and its application to low-cost automation, machinery attachments, work aids and methods of control.

Knitted fabric suppliers

The supply of warp knitted and of woven fabrics presents the industry with two very different problems.

Warp knitters have been closely associated with the increased use of filament nylon fibre in recent years and the warp knitted fabric trade is, from the shirt manufacturers' point of view, strong at the very point at which the woven cloth trade is least able to meet its requirements. A large proportion of the fabric it produces is used as shirting — over 30 per cent in 1968, compared with the 4 per cent of the output of the woven cotton trade. The home warp knitters appear able to lead the market in design, construction and colour, and yet also to provide good service in terms of quality, price and delivery.

It is not easy to foresee how the situation will develop. At the moment, with over half of the shirts worn in the UK made of warp knitted filament nylon, the country probably uses a higher proportion of nylon fibre than any other major shirt user. However, the notable improvements now being made in pure cotton shirtings, together with the rapid growth of interest in the various polyester/blends, make it unlikely that nylon's predominance will continue. It also appears likely that weft knitted shirting

44

fabrics, single and double jersey, will become more evident in the future, and in this type of fabric the emphasis may well be on spun polyester and polyester blends rather than on filament nylon. It remains to be seen how well the weft knitters can serve the home shirt industry although at present, the range of weft knitted fabrics supplied to other sectors of the clothing trade is very wide, and this sector of the knitting trade is expanding rapidly.

Quality

For purposes of definition, the essential elements in the quality of a shirt may be described as:

(a)   the physical weight of the cloth and its construction, design and finish

(b)   the inherent strength of construction of the garment, the regularity of the stitching, and the suitability of the interlinings and trimmings

(c)   the generosity of cut, and the manner in which the shirt fits

(d)   the degree to which the shirt retains its initial appearance, colour, crispness and fit, after reasonable wear and washing.

By and large, UK manufacturers are proud of the quality of their shirts, and indeed have a reputation in this country for quality. They should have no difficulty in maintaining the correct quality levels required by their markets in the future. They tend, however, to be critical of the quality of shirts made by competitors at home and abroad. Their opinions in this respect are difficult to justify, and it would appear that in fact there is little difference in the quality standards between equivalent manufacturers in the established shirt producing countries; each can produce a variety of quality standards if it sets out to do so. This is not to say that in certain markets, the USA for example, quality standards are very different from those generally accepted in the UK; in general, the local shirt industry adapts itself to the peculiar requirements of its home market, and carries a reputation for quality largely consistent with its home demands.

Future membership of the EEC

Future membership of the EEC was revealed by the study to be a potential advantage, as it would bring the UK shirt industry a much larger effective 'home' market, while still offering some protection against other overseas competition. If it could adapt itself to a new and changing environment, the industry could be in a position to become a leader in the fashion-conscious sector of the European market.

7.2 The weaknesses of the industry

The industry suffers likewise from several weaknesses, in relation to its overseas competitors, which must be assessed before any plan for its future can be drawn up.

Facilities for large scale production

Apart from the few companies mainly engaged in long run production, the UK does not have the same heritage of large, highly efficient, large scale manufacturing units as Hong Kong, and to a lesser degree, Portugal. The establishment of units of this type would indeed have been difficult, and to some extent undesirable, in the environment created by the history of the home industry and by the characteristics of its management and labour. For example, the type of female worker employed in the UK is not attracted to the large individual plants working one and a half or even two shifts on large scale production which form the backbone of the Hong Kong industry. Again, the heritage of plant is not readily convertible into very large units able to compete technologically with overseas manufacturers. Many of the buildings could not be easily extended or modified, and some factories are in areas where it would be difficult to find more labour of the right quality. Much of the management in the UK industry is not skilled, or interested in the techniques of large scale production, being more interested in variety and design innovation.

Woven cloth suppliers

The woven cloth trade as a whole seems to have actively set its sights on becoming competitive with overseas manufacturers in large scale production, and the Textile Council's recent study of the future of cotton and allied textiles in the UK put forward recommendations to make the 'cotton' textile industry fully competitive internationally in large scale production within a few years. But such pressures to build up long-run, round-the-clock production units are at the expense of the more specialised, shorter-run side of the business, with the result that shirting manufacture has largely declined, and the woven shirt manufacturers, being unable to obtain the quality and variety they need, are often forced to import. In 1968, only some 4 per cent of the total output of the woven 'cotton' trade in the UK was in the form of shirting fabrics.

Even the larger vertically-integrated groups, with interests in both cloth and shirt production, have apparently failed to overcome the problem. Their cloth-producing interests have become relatively large and capital intensive, concentrating on bulk production to the detriment of their shirt manufacturing interests.

In the opinion of many of the home shirt producers, the UK's woven shirting manufacturers, with few exceptions, suffer, moreover, from a paucity of aesthetic flair and design expertise. They appear to fail to provide shirt manufacturers with attractive designs backed by adequate samples, and even when the designs are acceptable, the service provided in the selected cloths is often unsatisfactory. Hence, the increasing reliance, already noted (2.5), of leading shirt manufacturers on Continental sources, especially Austria, Switzerland and Italy, and even on the USA, not only for innovation in design but often for supplies of the more standard classes of woven shirtings.

This is in direct contrast to conditions in the USA where the shirting market, by its size and demand for fashion, is highly attractive to the cloth manufacturers. There, and also in West Germany, a number of woven shirting suppliers make it their business to provide the individual shirt manufacturer with their most attractive lines, thus strengthening their home shirt manufacturers' ability to meet the market demands for more stylish and fashionable shirts.

Machinery supplies

The lack of a strong home-based industry supplying machinery and attachments to the UK shirt manufacturers puts them at a disadvantage, as compared with, for example, the USA, Japan, West Germany and Italy. Hong Kong is in a similar position to the UK in being forced to buy much of its shirt making equipment abroad, but its high level of capital investment in new shirt manufacturing units has attracted the keen attention of equipment suppliers with whom effective and lasting contact has been established. In the UK the rate of capital investment in the shirt industry appears to have lagged behind that of the USA and West German companies, due – it is reported by a number of home manufacturers – to lack of confidence in prospects for the future. This has meant that the UK industry has been rather slower than some of its overseas competitors in introducing new or improved methods of constructing and handling shirt components and complete garments. While the productivity trend has flattened off over the last two or three years in the UK (Figure 3.4), production efficiency has increased steadily in some overseas shirt industries better served by plant suppliers. It is not to be implied that there are no reliable and modern machinery suppliers in this country and no companies in the van of some specific aspect of shirt manufacture. But, on the whole, the level of effective communication and understanding between the shirt industry and its machinery suppliers could well be improved by both sides, and this would help to ensure a greater rate of technological progress and operating efficiency in UK shirt manufacture.

Chapter 8 Current market trends

There is a strong trend, particularly among young people, towards fashion in shirts, but the industry is not at present organised to benefit from it. Other current trends are towards higher-priced shirts – which include most of the fashion shirts – and towards polyester/cotton at the expense of nylon as a material

8.1 The demand for fashion

Your future in clothing pointed to a trend, spearheaded by young people, towards increased fashion consciousness in all clothing markets. In menswear it would seem to have been responsible for increasing the growth of the shirt market, which in recent years has shown itself to be responsive to the introduction of new products and fashion ideas.

Fashion in menswear tends to be concentrated on the individual garment, rather than the whole outfit, with flamboyance of both styling and cloth design the main feature. Shirts are among the 'trendiest' of all menswear items, apart from accessories, and they are produced in greater variety and are cheaper than most other items of outerwear. Few men will take a chance in fashion with an item costing £15 or more, but many feel able to risk buying a shirt at a fifth of the price, even though it may become out of fashion fairly soon.

Menswear, however, does not at present follow the trends occurring in some other fashion markets where change can occur at two levels, with possibly seasonal changes of colour and styling detail, and less frequent changes in the overall garment design.

Home manufacturers are thus protected to some extent from the competition of low-cost producers abroad. It is riskier for the retailer to order fashion items from overseas, where delivery may take longer than from home manufacturers who should be able to supply them more rapidly. This cuts down the commercial risk of making and purchasing unsaleable – ie, unfashionable – stocks of cloth for the manufacturer and finished garments for the retailer.

A syndicated fashion system by which shirt producers would present an emphasis on selected colours, styles and designs at one time in place of the current fashion free-for-all, would bring similar benefits. Such a system has already met with success in the USA, where the largest branded manufacturers are selling fashion vigorously; a recent fashion in bulk lines is 'deep' colours. The effects there have been to increase the public's interest in all shirts and to lessen the dependence of the larger retailers on imports from abroad. Similar trends are discernible in the UK – for example promotion on a limited scale of the 'Irish shirt' and the 'Northern Irish Shirt'.

8.2 The trend towards higher-priced shirts

A trend apparent in the past three years has been a shift in demand towards the more expensive types of shirt, as shown by Table 8.1. It is consistent with the gradual trading up by both manufacturers and retailers evident over a number of years by which prices have continued to rise steadily, albeit largely in discrete steps from one fixed price point to the next.

Although the price ranges quoted do not correspond exactly with the commodity, medium-quality and specialist shirt groups already discussed, most of the cheaper shirts, selling at up to 29s 11d will be of the commodity type, whilst those selling at between 30s and 50s will be mainly medium-quality garments, the specialist shirts being more expensive.

Table 8.1 Breakdown of shirt market by retail price (percentage units)

	1967	1968	1969
Up to 19s 11d	11	8	7
20s to 29s 11d	23	24	21
30s to 39s 11d	27	27	28
40s to 49s 11d	24	21	17
50s and above	15	20	27
Total	100	100	100

Source: ICI Fibres Ltd

The present market for the cheaper shirts — those priced at up to 29s 11d — is largely supplied from abroad, as UK manufacturers find it increasingly difficult to compete on price. Limits to its future development, however, are set by distribution problems — the traditional retailer finds it difficult to operate on the necessarily small margins and is losing business to the supermarkets and direct wholesalers — and by the evident low quality of the garments. Even in this cheap sector there are signs of trading up, which could become more marked when decimalisation allows stores to change some of the traditional price points.

Almost a third of the medium price market — shirts priced at from 30s to 49s 11d — is served by Marks and Spencer. That company's success lies in working together with a small group of efficient shirt producers to provide good-quality garments which are sold through a highly efficient retailing organisation operating on lower margins than most other retailers; other chain stores often have to buy from abroad if they are to compete in value for money with Marks and Spencer. Certain other shirts, of lower quality, owe their position in the medium price range to attractive packaging and their distribution through such channels as mail order and direct wholesale. Retailers' own brands are also often sold in this range, but this section of the market is vulnerable to stronger selling by the branded manufacturers.

The higher-priced end of the market — shirts priced at 50s and above — has shown the greatest growth in recent years. Most of the leading advertised brands fall into this price bracket. It is also the range in which the most fashion-sensitive garments — for example shirts with bright colours, bold designs and exaggerated individual styling — are primarily found. There is a clear evidence that a section of the public demands this type of shirt and is prepared to pay for it. The higher-priced end of the market may well continue to grow at a faster rate than the rest for the next few years; many of the consumers will be the fashion-conscious young people, with more money to spend on clothes than older people, and promotion will need to be geared accordingly.

8.3 The trend toward polyester blends

Table 8.2 shows a breakdown of the shirt market by fibre type as it was in 1968 and 1969, according to ICI Fibres, together with an estimate of the position in 1973, based on impressions of the likely market trends gained from contacts with manufacturers, customers and fibre suppliers at home and abroad.

There are several reasons for supposing that polyester blends will increase their share at the expense of nylon, despite the apparent setback to the fibre in 1969, which, it is believed, resulted from incorrect identification by consumers, due to its similarity to cotton. While offering similar wash and wear characteristics to nylon, polyester cotton shirts are considered by many consumers to be more comfortable and to look better, and have the appeal of a new product. They still pick up more dirt than nylon or cotton due to static, but the problem is being overcome with improved cloth finishes.

Table 8.2   Breakdown of shirt market by fibre (percentage)

Description	1968	1969	1973 (forecast)
Nylon	53	51	40
Polyester/cotton	6	4	20
Cotton	38	42	37
Other	3	3	3

Although nylon shirts are likely to retain some price advantage for the next few years at least, the price of polyester/cotton shirts will come down with the greater availability of the man-made fibre, as competition increases and in particular some form of warp knitting, as well as weft knitting, of the fibre becomes economic. Meanwhile, cotton cotton shirts will probably hold their proportion of the market but become more expensive.

After the mid 1970s, nylon is generally expected to lose further ground and the two man-made fibres may well share the market in equal proportions with cotton shirts.

Part 3 Prospects for the future

Chapter 9   Planning for growth

The market has shown itself capable of reacting to the introduction of new garments and fabrics, and opportunities exist for the UK industry to take the initiative with regard to both its suppliers and customers. If this is done, the home market could expand at 4–5 per cent per year to some 94 million units by the mid 1970s and to around 110 million by 1979, with UK shirt production and imports rising at the same rate, and exports slightly faster.

Growth will require positive industry and company planning: the industry is recommended to set up a comprehensive information service, perhaps with government assistance, and individual companies should clearly identify their chosen sectors of the market and, utilising modern planning techniques, plan all their activities accordingly.
Increased government protection from imports should not be required.

9.1 The potential for growth

Recapitulating on the current position in the home market, which takes some 95 per cent of the output of the UK shirt producers at present, the following salient points emerge:

The total market in numbers of units sold has grown at a reasonably steady rate of some 3.6 per cent per year over the past ten years (1.2).

Higher priced shirts have tended to account for a growing proportion of the home market in recent years (8.2).

The market has shown itself responsive to stimulation by new products and fibres, as demonstrated by the impact of the warp knitted nylon shirt in the early and mid 1960s (2.2).

The home producers are more competitive in economic terms in the UK market for medium-quality shirts than in the commodity shirt sector, in which the impact of the lower labour costs of certain overseas producers largely price out the home produced garments, even if they are manufactured in a development area or in Northern Ireland (6.5).

There is pressure from certain overseas suppliers, notably Portugal, Eire and Hong Kong, to sell shirts in the UK market – not only in the cheaper, commodity range, but also at the bottom end of the medium-quality bracket (2.2).

Much of the growing fashion awareness of the public in medium and high priced shirts has resulted from the activities not of shirt producers but of fibre suppliers (eg ICI Fibres) and the larger retail outlets (eg Marks and Spencer) (4.3, 4.4).

Bearing these factors in mind, it is forecast that if the UK shirt industry takes action to exploit its present position and its inherent strengths (7.1), it should be able to stimulate an increased rate of market growth, on the assumption that the UK economy continues to develop in a similar manner to recent years.

Figure 9.1 illustrates the forecast growth rate of the home market which, it is believed, is realistic if the industry takes the opportunities open to it at the present.

On this basis a market growth rate of between 4 per cent and 5 per cent is forecast, so that in volume terms, the total market, which in 1969 was 71 million shirts (1.1), will expand to some 94 millions by the mid 1970s and reach about 110 millions by 1979. Home production and imports will each maintain its present share and thus expand at a similar rate, as shown in Figure 9.1; exports, it is assumed, will rise at a slightly faster rate but still only reach about 7½ per cent of the total UK output by the mid 1970s.

Exploiting such opportunities to the full will require vigorous planning (discussed in this chapter), marketing with fresh initiative (Chapter 10), the improvement of manu-

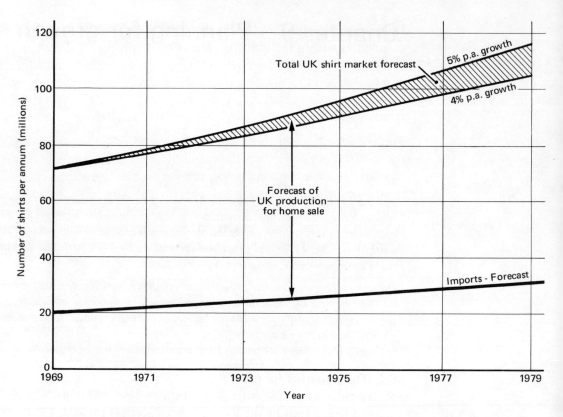

FIGURE 9.1 — FORECAST POTENTIAL GROWTH RATES FOR UK SHIRT MARKET

facturing processes (Chapter 11), a changed structure for the industry (Chapter 12), and revised requirements in capital and manpower (Chapter 13).

This growth rate is about twice the rate forecast by *Your future in clothing*, in which, it was considered that there was scope for growth in the shirt sector, but that it would be limited to 2 to 2½ per cent per year by the overall rigidity of clothing expenditure and the effect of large retail buyers who would tend to reduce the level of fashion consciousness by concentrating on a smaller range of garments and so lessening the need for variety; imports would run at a high level, supplying the additional shirts demanded by the market, so that home production would remain almost static. Such indeed might be the level of growth, if the industry failed to respond positively to its current opportunities.

9.2 Planning by the industry
If the industry is to influence and even dictate market changes, rather than merely respond to them, then it must take a positive initiative in planning, both as an industry and on a company basis.

A single industry plan cannot be presented in detail since individual companies' plans will tend to overlap, especially where they are competing in the same market sector. Nevertheless, there are several ways in which the industry can act in a united manner to influence its future.

One most important way is in the collection and dissemination of information about the market, its current position and anticipated trends. From the third quarter of 1970 the Board of Trade's *Business Monitor* will provide market size data on all companies employing 25 or more people, which, with the import data from the Customs and Excise, will enable a clear picture of the current market position to be drawn up. It must here be stressed that it is in the industry's own interests for companies to file their statutory returns quickly and comprehensively, for only then can the resulting market data be factual and up to date.

An additional source, of largely financial information, are the returns to the Registrar of Companies which now have to be filed by all except (in practice) the smallest companies, under the Companies Act of 1967, a sample of which is given in Figure 3.6.

In time, they will be invaluable as a basis for general comparison for the various companies within the industry, although it is recognised that an accurate inter-firm comparison cannot be derived from company accounts, and should be useful not only as a background to planned structural changes such as mergers and groupings by the members of the industry, but also as a means of attracting capital into the industry from outside.

To take advantage of these and other sources of information, it is recommended that the industry sets up a central organisation for collating the data and circulating it regularly to member companies, and for building up, from information supplied by companies, within or associated with the industry, information on such market criteria as the pattern of distribution and a breakdown of the market by price and garment type. This central body, having different functions, would preferably be separate from, although possibly sponsored by, the Shirt, Collar and Tie Manufacturers Federation, and indeed could be part of a combined organisation responsible jointly to it and to the Federations of other sectors of the clothing industry, or even, perhaps, to the clothing industry as a whole. Its employees, although responsible for separate sectors, would work as a combined team, sharing common facilities. The functions of the combined organisation would include devising the most effective means of handling information, standardising paperwork, carrying out or sponsoring specific market research within the industry, and if necessary purchasing information from other bodies such as the fibre suppliers who themselves conduct regular investigations.

The net result will be the establishment of a co-ordinated, reliable means of handling and interpreting market data, probably costing little more than the total of the sums spent for their own purposes by individual companies in the industry today. It would seem appropriate to seek government assistance in order to speed the setting up of the organisation, but routine operating costs will be borne by the industry.

Other ways in which the industry should effectively work as an entity are in the interpretation of the market's fashion demands, in encouraging companies to export, and in improving the industry's image in the eyes of its actual and potential employees.

9.3 Planning by individual companies

While it is not practicable in a report on an industry to make specific proposals to suit all companies or even all types of company, certain general recommendations can be made on planning at the company level to enable each organisation to seize the opportunities open to it, in the context of the industry's development as a whole.

(a)   A company will need first to identify its role in the changing market situation. It will then be able to recognise the various pressures to which it is likely to be subjected, and decide upon the pattern of its development most appropriate for the future. A detailed understanding of the limits and characteristics of its particular segment of the market will set guide lines for the types of product, the marketing policy, and production requirements in terms of quantity and quality for the company. It will enable the company to direct and foresee market changes and plan its operations accordingly. The company will also obtain some idea of the degree of risk involved, and thus of the likely stability of its future activities. Failure to define effectively the role of the company could lead to a dilution of effort throughout the organisation, with the result that the company might carry out a wide range of activities less effectively, rather than operating more successfully in a concentrated market area.

(b)   It should plan the overall level of its activities to at least equal the potential growth of the relevant market sector, unless a more radical growth is desirable for other reasons. This will ensure that the company does not lose ground to its competitors or influence with its suppliers and customers. In order to obtain the best possible understanding of its own markets, the company will need to make use of all available data, including that supplied by the central information group discussed above (9.2).

(c)   It should maintain a system of reasonably frequent appraisals to ensure that it is kept well aware of its changing assets and how it is using them. They should cover not only basic resources such as capital and manpower, but information on, for example, the rate of growth, changing pattern of customers, level of capital investment, gearing, level of capital intensity, and labour requirements. If necessary, outside resources may be called in to initiate the system. In some cases, it will be no more than an extension to an existing management information and accounting system, whilst in others staff will have to be made aware for the first time of such important indicators of their company's performance.

(d)   It should make specific plans, utilising modern corporate planning techniques, for the future deployment of its assets to meet requirements in marketing, production, manpower and finance.

(e)   Companies should make adequate plans for management succession at the highest levels, bearing in mind, again, changing requirements as both the company and its market develop. Chapter 12 points out that smaller and medium sized companies have a difficult problem here, as the leading executive may be the only man in the organisation with any total appreciation of the company as a whole; and it is accentuated by the fact that most similar companies in the clothing industry will be in an identical position. Companies should endeavour to anticipate the difficulty, and plan progressive careers to enable suitable men from within the company or outside to rise to top positions.

In short, every company is recommended to initiate an aggressive marketing policy for the future, backed by a corporate plan for making best use of its assets within the context of the planned growth of the industry. The policy will be strengthened by market data made available by the industry's information service recommended above.

9.4 The role of the Government
The shirt industry is not a large industry, measured against the total economy; it employs less than 0.1 per cent of the working population, has an unfavourable import/export trade balance, and provides garments of little strategic importance. Bearing in mind these limitations, it cannot expect more than average interest or protection from the Government; however, it is in a position to ensure a prosperous future for itself, in addition to making a continuing contribution to the national economy. The onus for planning, then, would appear to rest squarely on the industry itself, as would the responsibility for requesting Government action where this seemed appropriate.

Two factors have emerged during the study which relate to the proposed change from a quota to a tariff basis for the control of imports of cotton cloth and garments from the Commonwealth in 1972. Firstly, the most attractive opportunities for the UK industry lie in the medium-quality and speciality market areas, in which imported cotton garments are likely to be of little importance; secondly, in the cheap commodity shirt area, despite the fact that the home producers are not able to compete on price with the lowest labour cost importers, the current quota from Hong Kong, for example, is by no means filled at present, and the total level of imports of shirts of this type appears to be levelling off.

Thus, the change from the apparently unfilled quota to a tariff should have little effect on the larger part of the industry; the tariff, although it is reputed to be little more than many Hong Kong manufacturers are already paying to buy on to the quota, is approaching the general limit applied by GATT, and is not necessarily in line with the general trend to reduced tariffs recommended, for example, in the Kennedy Round discussions. Furthermore, a 'protected' environment for the UK industry would weaken the incentive for individual companies to improve their production and marketing methods, which would be against the industry's long-term interests. It is better for the home industry to strengthen its position in sectors of the home market which it can continue to dominate, and force potential overseas competition to seek other export markets by guiding the home market away from product types in which the low cost importers are most competitive.

Chapter 10   Marketing with initiative

More aggressive marketing by the industry is one of the key factors in its future growth. Manufacturers of retailers' brands will need to take some initiative in design, as well as improving their efficiency and their service. The fashion lead should be set by the branded manufacturers, who can influence the medium- and higher-priced areas of the market by establishing a syndicated fashion policy, setting up their own merchandising department, and increasing their advertising and promotion efforts. The smaller manufacturers should concentrate on exclusive, high fashion shirts.

Diversification, into other menswear items or into womenswear, could well be considered where this will not detract from the efficiency of companies' shirt interests.

10.1 Overall aims

At the present time it would appear that many UK shirt manufacturers not only fail to exploit their greatest inherent marketing strengths – proximity to the home market and creative ability (7.1) – but are negative in their attitude to marketing. The marketing initiative has been surrendered both to their cloth suppliers and to their customers: many companies derive much of their design and styling for both cloth and garments from overseas, and large retail organisations often play a bigger part than the manufacturers in defining standards of quality and design.

To break out of this position, individual manufacturers and the industry as a whole need to adopt more aggressive marketing policies. They will be aided by the revised structure of the industry, discussed in Chapter 12, in which large companies, able to deal on more equal terms with both suppliers and customers, will have a prominent place. Some suggestion of the possibilities open to manufacturers has already been given in Chapter 4, where it was pointed out that in America, where branded shirt manufacturers spend about twice as much of their total turnover on advertising as do companies in the UK, the number of shirts purchased per consumer each year is over twice that in the UK.

10.2 Syndicated fashion

The adoption of some form of syndicated fashion system, for which the opportunity already exists (8.1), should be a main feature of the new approach to marketing. The industry as a whole should aim to put across a basic 'look' in shirts each season – to develop a fashion conscious industry, with a recognisable pattern of style, design and colour at any one time. Companies should act as consumer goods manufacturers and sell positively to the real consumer, the public. Here, their closeness to the home market will help them to interpret what is acceptable, although selling will require care and delicacy, as it is generally accepted in marketing circles that the public resents the tendency of suppliers to dictate fashion.

Many advantages are likely to follow, if the shirt manufacturers succeed in organising themselves as a fashion industry. Regaining the initiative will create a mood of greater confidence and improve morale within the industry and recruitment of first-class managers will be easier. Manufacturers will be safeguarded against low-cost imports, as the UK will be making products that are not easy to buy from abroad without risk and which home buyers will therefore have good reason to purchase. Above all, the awakening of consumer interest in shirts will stimulate market growth, and the battle for a large part of the future shirt market will be fought on ground favouring the home producer, not the importer of mass produced cheap goods.

Three main problems will however face the industry. First, a suitable forum for setting up the syndicate will have to be established. This Report is not the place for recommending how this should be done, as voluntary co-operation is most effective when it results from the initiative of the participants. But the Shirt, Collar and Tie Manufacturers Federation might serve as a suitable starting point for the exchange of views and as a temporary venue for co-ordinating marketing strategy. Whatever the means, urgent action is recommended in this matter.

The second problem is posed by the relative weakness of home woven cloth suppliers (7.2). The UK and Europe are most likely to be the future sources of finished cloth in reasonable quantities for a fashion conscious industry, with the USA a possible source, especially of new ideas and fibres. UK warp knitters offer a good service and imaginative designs within the limits of the process and the nylon filament fibre which they largely use at present, at costs broadly acceptable to the shirt manufacturers and in time it may well be possible to warp knit polyester blends satisfactorily. UK woven cloth suppliers, however, are less well placed to supply the shirt industry against competition: they provide only limited and traditional designs, and as already inferred this is inadequate for a fashion market. There is no quick solution to this problem, although the growth of the syndicated fashion approach may well lead to an improvement in service. Entry into the EEC would make some European woven cloth sources more attractive than at present.

The third problem lies in the acceptance of the more fashion conscious image by the retailers. The large retailers will not necessarily find the fashion trends in their best interests in the light of their own moves towards larger scale purchasing of broadly similar ranges in order to economise on buying and stockholding costs. The industry must thus ensure that fashion influence spreads as far across the market as possible. This will thus involve selling to retailers by the most appropriate modern techniques, possibly involving them in the united fashion front, and increasing the pressure exerted by the shirt manufacturers on the final consumer — by advertising, for example, either in their own right or in conjunction with fibre or material suppliers.

10.3 Manufacturers of retailers' brands

Large suppliers of retailers' own brands of shirt manufacture to a specification which, depending on the retailer, may or may not be strictly defined. Manufacturing to their customers' orders, they do no marketing in a creative sense, although while they are retained as suppliers, their sales are assured. Their marketing efforts should therefore be directed towards safeguarding their position vis-à-vis their customers, the retailers.

These bulk manufacturers are in direct competition with overseas suppliers, whose wage costs are lower and with whom it is difficult to compete on price alone. Evidence suggests that retailers will pay no more than a 10 per cent premium for UK-made shirts of equal quality to an overseas produced garment. The following recommendations are intended to lessen the vulnerability of manufacturers selling by this channel. Many are self-evident but are included in the Report for completeness.

(a)   The manufacturer should make every effort to reduce costs by adopting the measures recommended in Chapter 11 for increasing productivity, becoming more capital-intensive, etc. He should work with the customer on the specification of the shirt to ensure that he can manufacture it as effectively as possible, while retaining its basic consumer qualities; only in this way can he gain room for manoeuvre in price negotiations with customers. When planning extra capacity, he should consider the case for moving to a development area, where there are considerable savings to be made in production costs, provided that labour and management problems can be overcome (5.3).

(b)   Service to the customer should be above criticism: shirts should at least meet the customer's quality standards, and any complaints should be handled promptly. Only feasible delivery dates should be promised, and, if they cannot be met owing to circumstances beyond his control, the customer should be warned as early as possible; here, his closeness to the market gives the UK manufacturer an advantage over his overseas competitors. He should be able to anticipate his customer's quantity requirements, in time to engage and train new operators for increased production.

(c)   He should take some initiative in design, and promote an interest in fashion in as much of his merchandise as possible. He must keep abreast with fashion trends, supply samples, and set up his production unit so that fashion shirts can be produced economically.

(d)   He should spread his risks by increasing the number of his customers, but any increase in size or changes in his organisation should not be allowed to affect adversely his service to each customer.

10.4 Manufacturers with their own brands

The manufacturers of the well-known advertised brands should take the lead in setting the syndicated fashion trend by establishing a clearly defined product policy for themselves and setting a lead for the industry as a whole. Only in this way can the maximum impact be concentrated where it matters – on the consumer. The fashion will, in general, outline the basic colours and design features at any one time, individual brands being distinguished by styling differences and other subtle factors which give each an identifiable 'hallmark'.

As suggested above (10.1), fashion co-ordination within the industry should result from action by the manufacturers themselves. Within the companies, the procedure for selecting ranges for merchandising should in many cases be overhauled. In place of the committee or even the single individual who in many companies has this task, the larger manufacturers should set up small but influential merchandising departments like those in the larger American shirt companies. A department's task will be to interpret fashion trends for its company so that it can produce acceptable, fashionable shirts in long enough runs to be profitable. A probable benefit will be that many manufacturers will be able to cut down on the variety of styles and designs offered – a trend that will be enhanced by the growth in size of many shirt manufacturers; fewer, larger suppliers to a given market will result in a reduced total number of ranges available, which will in fact ease the problem of controlling a syndicated fashion trade.

Close co-operation with cloth suppliers and retailers will be necessary, but the main selling effort should be concentrated on the consumer, which of course will be in the retailer's interest as well as the manufacturer's. With this in mind, branded manufacturers will need to spend more heavily on advertising and promotion. Bearing in mind the characteristics of the American shirt market, the level and methods of advertising in related fields in the USA, and the actual size of the leading shirt producers in that country, it is recommended that the leading branded UK manufacturers should step up their advertising budgets to something approaching the American level of some 6 per cent of turnover; even at their present size, three or four of the larger companies would at this level spend enough to make a worthwhile impact on consumers in the UK.

Branded manufacturers should try to extend their distribution to cover outlets such as multiple tailors which do not as yet handle shirts in any quantity but are moving into shirts to an increasing extent. The experience of the grocery trade in covering more and more retail outlets with fewer selling points would repay examination; for example, the provision of a stock replacement service on a regular basis. Also, branded manufacturers may well find themselves better able to capture some of the retailers' own-label business with their increased marketing strength; the major problem of maintaining deliveries when demand for their own products is high can only be overcome by forward planning, based on a good knowledge of likely market trends in the near future, and, in this, the setting up of the industry wide information service recommended in Article 9.2 will be valuable.

10.5 Marketing by the smaller company

The only viable position for the small UK shirt manufacturer is likely to be at the top end of the market where there will be scope for specialist services that large manufacturers would have difficulty in providing. A more fashion conscious environment in the bulk of the market may well increase the demand for the real exclusiveness which only the small companies can provide. Their aim therefore should be to market high fashion shirts, preferably in a well-defined field – very much as is done by some existing companies. As a further step to exclusiveness, their retail distribution should probably be restricted to selected outlets. The shirts, because of their high fashion content, will carry greater risk than those of the larger companies, and pricing policies should reflect this fact. Advertising and promotion, although important, will be less so than for the larger companies. Their small size can thus become a source of strength. But if a small company grows then its advantage is lost, unless it is prepared to change its character and operate as a medium sized organisation. There is obviously scope for limited growth for all companies, but the necessity for continued growth is less critical for the efficient small company.

In line with the development of a united fashion front by a number of the larger manufacturers (10.2), there is scope for several smaller shirt producers to join in making common use of a leading designer, for cloth or garments, thus obtaining a measure of design excellence whilst preserving their individuality. At the other end of the market, a somewhat precarious existence will remain possible for small manufacturers of retailers' own brands — mainly supplying fill-in orders from retailers unable or unwilling for particular reasons to buy their full requirements from overseas; the risks of this class of business for the small manufacturer will be high, and the financial returns limited.

10.6 Diversification

Diversification of interests is an option open to all manufacturers, regardless of size and can be justified not only as a safeguard against recession in a particular market sector, but as a means of gaining expertise from another, probably related, sector of industry. Shirt companies in the USA are diversified to a marked degree, and only the smaller and more exclusive manufacturers make and sell shirts only. The larger, in addition, either sell or make and sell most kinds of menswear accessories and outerwear, and all have thriving womenswear divisions. They are also active in retailing, and three of the largest companies own extensive chains of retail outlets — mostly department stores rather than menswear shops. Some of the smaller shirt companies have themselves been taken over as part of other companies' diversification programmes. West German companies by and large are not diversified to such an extent, but Swedish and the larger Portuguese shirt companies make and sell other types of garment, for both men and women.

The possibilities open to UK manufacturers are narrower, since a proportion of the shirt industry is already owned by groups who have other interests in clothing. Diversification for the majority would have to be in related fields. The following suggestions are based on visits in the UK and overseas and not on any detailed study of all the diversification prospects open to the UK companies.

(a) Diversification into other items of menswear would spread selling overheads over a larger turnover and enlarge the opportunities for putting over co-ordinated fashions. Ties are an obvious line as the buying channels are similar but knitwear, trousers and the entire leisure-wear field could be considered. This type of diversification would demand, as well as good merchandising, careful formulation of selling policy and methods.

(b) Women's clothes would be a suitable field for shirt companies with large production units, prepared to manufacture a variety of lines; their expertise in manufacturing indeed would be of great value, as many women's wear suppliers appear to be less efficient in production, their strength lying in extreme fashion awareness and the ability and willingness to respond to the market demands as rapidly and often as required. Marketing and selling of the merchandise would, however, dictate the profitability of the venture, and therefore would require exhaustive preliminary investigation.

Chapter 11 Efficiency in manufacture

To sustain the projected growth, manufacture will have to be made more efficient. Overall productivity can be significantly improved by the application of modern production and workplace engineering techniques. The industry must keep abreast with developments in automatic machinery and control methods, and improve its liaison with plant and equipment suppliers at home and abroad. Whilst co-operating with fibre and cloth suppliers in more basic research work, the industry should concentrate its own new thinking into such areas as improved marketing and operator job satisfaction as well as the development and application of modern production and control methods. It should moreover take part in moves to make more use of the research associations for co-ordinated research work.

11.1 Productivity

The attainable production rates given for costing purposes (5.2) exceed those achieved in practice by many UK companies. Productivity targets have in the past tended to be set too low, and thus to have been too easily satisfied. Indeed, the NEDO report *Attainable production targets** gives the average potential increase in output for a given number of operator hours as 48 per cent for the UK shirt industry as a whole. Provided that certain measures are put in hand, a really significant increase in productivity is therefore within the reach of many companies in the industry.

Productivity in a factory can very often be improved by the objective application of modern techniques of production engineering. A large company may have the resources to engage professional staff to make the necessary assessment, but the medium-sized or small company will have to rely on hiring advice from consultants; typically, the cost of consultants' fees to a medium-sized company with about 250 staff would be £15,000–£20,000, spread over about 18 months, for a complete analysis of all production activities.

Expenditure on advice will inevitably be accompanied by expenditure on plant and equipment. In the present state of development of stitching machinery, increased productivity is less limited by needle speeds than by handling time, so that the most worthwhile investment will be in workplace engineering. This term covers the provision of mechanical handling and workpiece presentation devices, and the spacial positioning of the operator and machine in the optimum position in relation both to other personnel in the production line and to the garment itself. Other promising areas for possible future investment are the design of an optimum factory layout making full use of the total volume of the building, and installation of the best system of workpiece progression at each stage of production — ie progressive bundle or continuous flow. Allied with workplace engineering will be an outlay on small parts and gadgets to speed up presentation and removal of the workpiece to and from the needle. As an example, the total cost, again in a factory employing 250 people, might amount to about £20,000, made up as follows:

Cutting room	£	200
Parts machining	£	4,000
Assembly machining	£10,000	
Finishing and packing	£	5,000
		£19,200

---

*Attainable production targets, 1969, HMSO 22s 6d

The annual financial benefits to the company as a whole, resulting from this combined expenditure on advice and workplace engineering of some £40,000 can be more than twice this amount if productivity is raised by the target of 48 per cent.

11.2 Equipment

There may also be scope for the installation of further automatic equipment in many shirt factories — in particular, machines for profile stitching collars and for button-holing shirt fronts. Although their capital costs are relatively high and UK manufacturers have criticised them as inflexible, they are already being used by many of the leading manufacturers in Sweden and Germany, and their use here should be justifiable on economic grounds, provided that adjacent operations are arranged to make full use of the new plant. In some cases increased levels of shift working on this equipment alone as applied in some factories in the USA and West Germany, may need to be considered. The more sophisticated machines apart, in this country there are interesting developments in progress on the application of low cost automation to such tasks as automatic sequence control. A group at the Ministry of Technology is actively working in this field with several UK companies, and it is anticipated that the applications of such techniques will be of great value, especially to the smaller manufacturer. For example, benefits which are particularly likely to accrue from fluidic control systems applied to machines are reduced training time and less operator fatigue, leading to increased production per operator.

The adoption of new machinery, however, is hindered by the poor liaison with suppliers already mentioned (7.2). Shirt manufacturers have to purchase most of the more advanced semi-automatic multi-operation machines from abroad, through agents, which places them at a disadvantage, both in terms of technical service and often of delivery. To remedy the situation, the larger shirt manufacturers could follow the example of their competitors overseas, particularly in the USA where machinery suppliers lend new equipment on trial, on condition that other potential users should be allowed to see the plant and have access to broad performance details. Similar advantages could be gained by encouraging UK manufacturers of sophisticated control equipment for machines to operate in the same manner. The plant manufacturers, abroad and at home, would be given in return full performance data on the trials, and kept fully briefed on deficiencies and on development possibilities; complaints about, for instance, the inflexibility of a machine could then be transferred into collaboration on its improvement. It should be noted however that the Ministry of Technology operates such a service under its Pre-Production Order Scheme where new and advanced British machinery, not yet made available, is bought and placed with users with an option to purchase. On a valuation by the user a report is issued describing the performance of the machine.

Another problem lies in the servicing of equipment and the construction and development of simple work aids. Unlike the USA and West Germany, for example, the UK does not appear to have an adequate supply either of small companies who specialise in the 'one off' job of this nature, or of skilled maintenance and development engineers who would be permanently employed by the larger manufacturer or possibly by a group of the smaller shirt manufacturers. Recommendations on the latter point are made in Chapter 13.

11.3 The scale and location of production

As has been shown (5.3), factories operating at below their economic production level — about 600,000 commodity shirts or 300,000 medium-quality shirts per year — could be enlarged to three or four times their present operating size and show cost savings. There is certainly a case for forming several of the present medium-sized companies into groups with single new production units, in a development area, preferably Northern Ireland.

Eire is another possible site for development, but could be deprived of its favourable position in the commodity shirt trade by the tariff on cotton shirts in 1972. If Eire and the UK enter the EEC together, Eire could become an attractive proposition for suppliers of the European and hence the UK market, although less so as local wage rates rise with improved living standards.

UK investment in overseas shirt manufacture, outside Eire, is rather less attractive, and the problems of industrial relations, training difficulties, and the uncertainty of the international financial position, appear to outweigh any potential economic advantage. Such problems are known to have been encountered by West German and Swedish investors in Portugal.

11.4 Research and development

Considerable concern is being expressed at present about the level of research and development in the clothing industry, which is low, when compared with that in the textile and other associated industries. Recent evidence presented to the Clothing EDC, revealed that 'only some £385,000 was being spent annually on research and development by the UK clothing industry, as opposed to a sum of some £12 million per annum in textiles'. Some of this was of course used to sponsor work done by organisations outside the industry; in this connection mention must be made of the recent investigation by the Shirley Institute into the cost of cloth faults in shirt manufacturing.

When seen in the full context of all manufacturing and marketing activity in clothing and fabric goods, it would seem more appropriate for the textile industry than the clothing industry to be involved in such subjects as the development of new fibres and fabrics, and methods of cloth construction and finish. However, if research and development is interpreted more precisely as investigation into the need for, and means of, development and application of new techniques, there are several fields in the clothing trade, especially the more promising sectors like the shirt industry, in which it could well be stepped up.

It is widely held that in any industry sector there are two extreme levels of research and development activity. If the industry is in a static environment and, for various reasons, does not wish to change the situation, then a minimum 'basic' level of new thinking can be justified. If, on the other hand, the industry is either in a rapidly changing situation or intends to adopt an increasingly aggressive stance in relation to its competitors, then a very much higher level of expenditure on research and development is called for. Thus, assuming the shirt industry takes the initiative, as implied in this Report, a big increase in its research and development budget will be essential to support its position vis-à-vis overseas competitors.

For the shirt industry, there are three main streams of investigation in which additional investment is required for the future, in addition to areas in which it will need to work in close co-operation with its suppliers.

Firstly, as the industry becomes increasingly aggressive in its marketing, it will need to be at the forefront of development of the techniques most relevant to its own products and customers. This will involve not only seeking to apply, and if necessary modify, the proved marketing methods of other comparable industries (eg consumer products, such as food), but also developing new marketing techniques appropriate to its own customers (eg specialised cash and carry and stock replacement services).

Secondly, in order to retain its work force in the face of increasing competition from other industries, the industry should investigate new ways of providing motivation and job satisfaction for its operators and management. At the operator level, this could involve the whole question of the balance of skill and craftsmanship against speed at repetitive operations, bearing in mind the varying level of capital investment associated with each method. The effects of multiple operation training and career planning as a means of improving job satisfaction should also be covered.

One facet of its industrial relations in which the shirt industry could well benefit from further research is the interaction between productivity and workers' relationships, with each other, with their immediate supervisors and with management. This is particularly relevant to the industry at the present time, as the character of management-labour relations is about to change with the coming of equal pay and the probable emergence of a few larger shirt manufacturers. In this, the UK industry should be able to draw on the work of such bodies as the Tavistock Institute of Human Relations and others who are already active in this field.

Thirdly, the industry should concern itself with improving production methods, in view of the changing situation created by machinery development on the one hand and by the rising cost of labour on the other. This would include a consideration of more sophisticated control methods, in terms of both actual machines and handling equipment, as well as devices for monitoring the quality of the work at various stages, for example. In these areas, the development work would involve the close liaison with manufacturers of equipment of all types, in addition to the cloth and fibre suppliers.

The few large companies envisaged in this Report will play an important part in all areas of research and development. Not only will they be more likely, by virtue of their size, to carry out their own research work than smaller firms, but they will be more inclined to support or sponsor external research, at the research associations and academic centres, where there is now a growing interest in textiles and clothing.

Chapter 12   The future shape of the industry

A reshaping of the industry's structure will need to accompany the improvements in planning, marketing and manufacturing if the industry is to take advantage of its opportunities. One main feature could be the emergence of a few very large companies, which not only would improve the image of the industry as a whole, but could themselves enjoy advantages in marketing, production and recruitment of management and labour beyond the scope of the largest existing companies. Medium sized companies would continue to handle a considerable volume of business but would be handicapped by their intermediate size. The small companies would decline in number, leaving the more successful who choose to remain small to concentrate on the speciality high-fashion trade. The total number of companies would fall by 40 per cent, and the average company size would more than double, by the mid 1970s.

12.1 The future structure

Within the scope of this study, it is not possible to consider in detail all the implications and interactions of the various strategic policies that the industry could follow; thus detailed forecasts of its future shape cannot be made with accuracy. Nevertheless, it is possible to suggest a structure which could emerge from the present situation if the industry were to exploit the opportunities open to it. On the basis of this suggested structure for the future, the likely trends in labour and capital requirements are discussed in Chapter 13.

The industry structure would be headed by a small number (perhaps four) of large companies, each with shirt manufacturing interests amounting to an annual turnover of £3.3 million to £10 million; these would be larger than the biggest single company in the industry today. They may well be part of larger groups outside the industry, if the association does not detract from their role as shirt manufacturers. No overall advantage (apart from the greater availability of finance) will result from belonging to groups with cloth supply or shirt retail outlets; such additional links can undoubtedly be used effectively, but will alter the pattern of external trading rather than influence its overall profitability, and to some extent spread the risk in times of recession in one sector. Some large companies may well be formed by amalgamations of present leading manufacturers with common interests in products or outlets. They will almost certainly dominate the better-quality branded shirt market, and together should act as leader to the rest of the home trade in improving quality, design and marketing.

Within the altered structure, there will continue to be a group of medium sized companies with turnovers between £330,000 and £3.3 million per year. They are likely to suffer disadvantages from being neither large nor small, which may well affect their long-term profitability, although they will still handle a considerable volume of products. Some will be companies who have remained of medium size for many years; others will be formed from erstwhile smaller companies by amalgamation or organic growth.

The present number of small companies, with annual turnovers of under £330,000, will gradually decline during the 1970s by amalgamation, diversification into other product areas or liquidation. There will still be a place for successful entrepreneurs, but problems of succession will reduce the number of small companies in the future.

Those remaining will concentrate on speciality high-fashion business, making full use of their individual flair and flexibility to create and meet the demands for their particular products. The postulated structure of the industry in the mid 1970s, which would enable it to take advantage of its potential, is compared diagrammatically with the 1969 structure, by size and volume of turnover, in Figures 12.1 and 12.2.

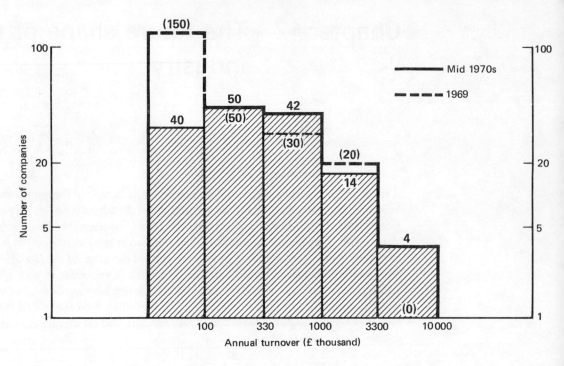

FIGURE 12.1 – THE FUTURE STRUCTURE OF THE INDUSTRY BY COMPANY SIZE

The total annual turnover in the mid 1970s is estimated as about £94 million, compared with £71 million in 1969, at manufacturers' prices, which are assumed to remain broadly constant in real terms, as has been the case over the past ten years. The position is summarised in Table 12.1.

Although this is by no means an accurate forecast of the exact future structure of the industry, it is evident that considerable changes can be foreseen for a number of companies, which in extreme cases could mean mergers, diversification or even liquidation. The decisions involved for the individual company are necessarily complex, and consideration should be given to the establishment of a specialised service providing professional advice on an impartial and confidential basis to companies undergoing radical change. A similar body has been recently sponsored by the Economic Development Committee for the wool textile industry, and the shirt industry might be well advised to become acquainted with its operations before taking positive action itself.

The respective strengths and weaknesses of the three sizes of company are summarised in the following Articles.

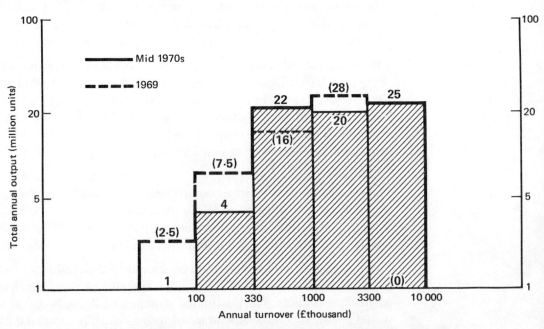

FIGURE 12.2 – THE FUTURE PATTERN OF COMPANY OUTPUT

Table 12.1 The future structure of the industry

	1969	Mid 1970s	Average per cent change per year
Total output (£m per year)	72	95	+ 4.5
Approximate no. of companies	250	150	− 9
Average company size (£m per year)	0.29	0.63	+ 14

12.2 Large companies

The large company will be particularly well placed to carry out many of the recommendations made in the report. In management, it will be able to attract from outside the industry men of the highest calibre, not only for its current top positions but for lower positions from which the leaders of the future can be promoted. By definition, there are few opportunities within the industry at present for men best suited to lead these larger organisations, since the qualities needed to manage a company with a £10 million per year turnover are very different from those of the head of a company one-tenth of its size, owing to the different responsibilities, motivation and method of working. At the same time, the large company will be well placed to carry out the comprehensive management training recommended in the next chapter (13.2), and its scale of operation will allow full use of advanced management and financial control techniques, including computer-aided methods (13.1).

In recruiting labour it will be able to offer attractive working conditions, wage structure and fringe benefits in competition with other industries employing mainly female personnel. In the light of the pressures to increase the formalisation of management-labour relations, the initiative in forging a satisfactory basis for these relationships will need to be taken by both management and unions in the larger companies, who will inevitably be looked to for leadership by the rest of the industry.

In marketing, too, the large company's potential will be very different from that of its smaller counterparts Again, it can attract the right class of men, both for the senior position at board level and, by virtue of its soundly-based marketing and selling organisation, in the lower positions offering prospects of promotion. It will have sufficient of the business in a particular field to play a major part in growth and development of its own particular markets. It can take the initiative in dealing with its suppliers, direct customers and the end users, and can exploit its capacity to advertise and promote on a worthwhile scale at home and even in selected overseas markets. A company of its size, furthermore, will be able to set up a specialised merchandising department with the functions recommended above (10.4).

In production, the large company will be able, if it chooses, to centralise the process control, laying, cutting, etc, and possibly the finishing, pressing, packing and stocking operations, leaving only actual machining operations to satellite units. It may, on the other hand, prefer to rely on individually controlled production units, each making a complete range of shirts ready for dispatch. The choice will depend on the range of products being made and on the availability of labour; but it is likely that by the mid 1970s the companies operating the central control and satellite system will be on the increase.

The large company should be able to command the direct interest of the best machinery suppliers. It should, with its size and breadth of experience, be able to work with its plant-makers on machinery and attachment development — which will help to command the suppliers' interest, as well as contributing to the advance of the technology of the industry as a whole.

Overall, the industry will benefit from the existence of a number of much larger companies, each operating efficiently and making full use of its size. The companies, and the leading men in them, could make a significant impact on the image which the industry presents to the world outside — an image which is created largely not by its products but by the reputation which the trade has by virtue of its standards of employment and management and, to some degree, its success. Although this image may not have a drastic influence directly on the purchases of home produced shirts, it could be vital in attracting capital, management and labour into the industry — all essentials for the future prosperity of the shirt industry.

12.3 Medium-sized companies

The medium-sized company may appear to have some of the potential advantages of the large company, but in practice it is not likely to be large enough to exploit them. It will tend to operate either as a large company at below optimum size, or as an over-large small company, trying to control an organisation too big for the methods employed.

In management, for example, its needs will be different from those of the large company, and the class of man who can be attracted and retained will be more limited. Too often the best man obtainable will be the good specialist who has proved himself as a production or sales manager or accountant, but who, when promoted, will run the company as a large production or sales unit, with less than the best results. The transition from specialist to general management is a difficult one; indeed, companies now in this turnover range should consider to what extent their operations are biased in this manner and how much their business as a whole suffers as a result. If the chief executive also has a controlling financial influence, further problems may arise — ones that will not trouble the large company normally run by a professional manager with a relatively small ownership stake in the business.

The medium-sized company may be less likely than the large company to be able to provide an attractive working environment for its employees and may suffer from a lack of suitable openings for key personnel.

Its marketing strength again will probably be below optimum, especially in advertising and promotion, but if it specialises in a particular product type or by serving a single group of customers, much of this disadvantage may be overcome. Organisational problems may beset its rather smaller sales effort, with adverse effects on the quality of personnel, although the incentive of a good salary in a fairly progressive company may attract the right men.

The production picture is similar, in that the medium-sized company, with its smaller number of production units — perhaps only two, or even one, in some cases, cannot be as flexible or resilient as the large company. It is less able to attract interest from machinery suppliers and to contribute to technological development in return.

In general, the medium-sized company will tend to suffer the worst of both worlds, and its management will be under considerable strain as a result. Ownership interests may well conflict with the right development plan for its future; and it is probable that the most successful companies of this size will either be those with a competent owner-executive or those employing perhaps slightly younger professional managers attracted by the potentially faster promotion rate or the prospects of more varied management experience than offered by the large organisation.

12.4 Small companies

Unlike the medium-sized company, the small company with an annual turnover of less than some £330,000 can take advantage of its limited size, and, unless it plans dramatic growth, function in a completely different manner.

A fundamental feature of the small company is that its success depends critically on the abilities of the man at the top, who runs what is often his own business, largely by his own expertise. The company's management problems are thus his, and, as he is responsible solely to himself, his decisions for the future are wholehearted and undisputed. The well-run small company under an energetic entrepreneurial owner-executive can, as a result, be highly efficient.

His dominance also strongly influences the marketing and production aspects of the small company. If he is production-oriented, the manufacturing will be of a high standard; similarly the marketing and selling, if these are his forte. The fact that the company may consequently be biased to one extreme or the other may not matter unduly, when the overall success of the company will be carried on his shoulders and will stand or fall with him.

The weakness of the small company is often the succession to the top position, which the owner-executive often fails to provide for. His demise may be disastrous for the company, especially when there is a shortage of ready capital to tide over a difficult period of readjustment. In such circumstances, the company may either be absorbed by a larger concern, amalgamate with another small company, or go out of business.

Chapter 13   The future needs of the industry

The capital required to finance new factories, replace plant and improve production methods may well approach some £14 million over the next five years. The industry should introduce more modern methods of financial appraisal and control, and of corporate planning, and consider further reductions in stock levels and increases in financial gearing ratios, especially for the independent companies.

In line with the forecast expansion, manpower requirements could fall by 15–20 per cent by the mid 1970s, during which time wages must be expected to rise annually by some 6 per cent in real terms, slightly faster than the anticipated average for clothing. There must be a greater emphasis on operator training, with career prospects, and the industry should consider training schemes for development and maintenance engineeers.

The larger organisations of the future will need to attract management from outside the industry and the textile industry's co-operation, both for management training within the industry and for the setting up of a common management training college should be sought.

13.1 Finance
The overall policies for future action already outlined enable an estimate of the industry's total requirements for capital by the mid 1970s to be made, as detailed in Table 13.1.

Table 13.1   Future capital requirements

Expenditure	£ million
New factories (plant and buildings)	3.5
Replacement of existing plant (£1 million per year)	6
Total (by mid 1970s)	9.5

The capital for new plant and building allows for some 50 per cent of the additional 23 million shirts produced by the mid 1970s (Figure 9.1) to be manufactured in the new factories. The capital expenditure estimate is based on a typical capital charge of some 15d per shirt, which is equivalent to a capital charges factor of 20 per cent per annum (see Appendix E). The capital allowed for replacement is an estimate of what might be necessary to maintain that part of the existing plant still in efficient use in the mid 1970s.

It is assumed that normal investment grants of 20 per cent will be obtained for new plant, although, allowing for delays in grant payments their value has been discounted for a period of six months at 12 per cent.

This total capital requirement covers the necessary expansions and plant replacement due to obsolescence entailed by the anticipated outputs. Further sums, required as companies proceed to implement other recommendations in this report such as the introduction of more sophisticated capital equipment or the movement of production facilities to areas more attractive from the cost point of view or to improve their production in the light of market or technical developments, may increase the total by some 50 per cent to some £14 million over the next five years. This sum includes investment allowances for buildings to house the expansion and allows for the fact that sophisticated control or management systems involving capital expenditure on such items as computers may result from the emergence of a few much larger companies in the 1970s.

The ability of the industry to raise finance will depend not only on companies' profitability records and capital structure, but on a third criterion, now becoming increasingly important – the calibre of their management and its plans for the future. Thus, apart from its other benefits, implementation of the report's recommendations on management (13.3) will assist the flow of capital into the industry.

The data available from Companies House (3.4) has shown that the gearing ratio for independent companies is very much lower than that for subsidiary companies, whose financial affairs are in general under group control. This may well be due to two causes: the recent credit restrictions and relatively poor average profitability within the trade, which would hit the independent, whose whole future is in shirts, rather more than a member of a group with widespread interests; and lack of appreciation of the advantage to a profitable company of raising new finance by way of fixed interest capital rather than equity.

The effect of increased gearing on the return on equity in a profitable company is illustrated in Figure 13.1, the average current gearing ratios for the independent and subsidiary companies who filed returns at Companies House (see Chapter 3) being shown.

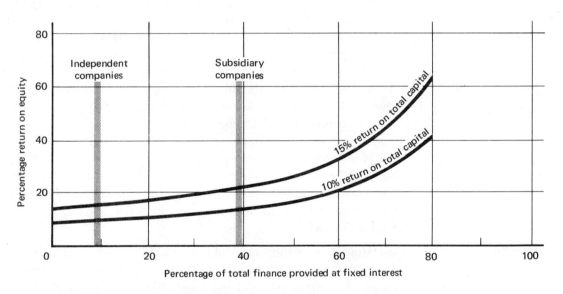

FIGURE 13.1 – THE EFFECTS OF GEARING ON RETURN ON EQUITY

Other factors being equal, the subsidiary companies are clearly in a more attractive position in terms of percentage return on equity with their considerably higher gearing.

In view of the fluctuating stock levels due to the seasonal nature of much of the shirt business and the consequent need for short term finance to cover them, a company's first priority is to decide on its minimum acceptable stock levels through the year, and then to consider its optimum gearing as and when new capital is required. Necessary conditions are that the level of profit and the cash flow situation are adequate to cover the interest payments, and that the short term debts can, in fact, be raised as required. Many companies in the industry have already decided upon and achieved a satisfactory gearing level, in line with their marketing policy and product range, but there may well be a number who have not yet fully appreciated the financial penalty entailed by seeking too high a proportion of their new capital in equity rather than at fixed interest.

On the question of loan capital, from discussion with a number of members of the industry, it is believed that the true cost of loan capital may not be fully appreciated. Allowing for Corporation Tax at 45 per cent, and an additional factor to account for the effects of inflation, which will depend on the actual end use to which the capital is applied, the true cost of the loan may well be reduced to less than half of its apparent value.

In assessing its financial future, each individual company should then decide precisely how the overall future trends and opportunities can best be interpreted in its own case. However, several general recommendations on the analysis of future investment apply to a greater or lesser extent to all future activity of this type. At the present many companies determine the estimated profitability of a new venture on a criterion of direct return on net assets, before tax. A more appropriate method, particularly where important investments are envisaged, is the use of discounted cash flow techniques, which have the advantage of taking into account the timing of the future cash flows; as requested by the Study Group, a brief description is given in Appendix C.

Many other techniques of investment appraisal have come into prominence in the last decade, and are becoming accepted as advanced business practice. An example is risk analysis, which, in view of the high risk element attached to much of the industry's activity, many companies would be well advised to undertake in some form. The merits of the techniques lie not only in their taking into account many more relevant factors than the older methods, but in entailing a greater discipline of forecasting and cost estimating, which in themselves provide a better understanding among a greater number of people of a company's true situation and prospects.

A vitally important factor is the rate of return which a company in the shirt trade should anticipate from a given future action. There is evidence from the data filed at Companies House that in the past many companies have worked on rates of return on net assets which are well below the norm of 20 per cent per year discussed in Article 3.4. This return broadly corresponds to a 10 per cent DCF return as shown in Appendix D, which is the minimum permitted for many nationalised industries. It must be stressed that this can only be regarded as an acceptable return for the least risky sectors of the shirt industry, and that many of the companies operating at the high risk, fashion-dependent end of the trade should regard returns of up to double the minimum recommended above as the lowest acceptable. The degree of risk depends not only on the element of fashion but on the level of effective competition, so that the company competing, for example, against imports in a semi-bulk commodity shirt market may well be facing a relatively high risk, especially if they are manufacturing retailers' brands.

Investment opportunities would seem to be open to efficient UK shirt manufacturers at a high standard of profitability; but if a company cannot justify such an investment, in its own long-term interests and those of the industry, the additional capital should be invested in a more profitable sector of the economy.

13.2 Manpower

Manpower requirements of the industry in the mid 1970s will be subject to several influences — the level of production, the processes used in manufacture, and to a lesser degree the methods used for purchasing, marketing, selling and other company activities, efficiency, and the average number of hours worked.

By the mid 1970s, the forecast output of the home industry will be some 94 million units, an increase of some 35 per cent on the 1969 level (9.1). Estimated improvements in labour productivity as outlined in *Attainable Production Targets* could be up to 48 per cent on existing performance (11.1); over the next five years, an improvement of some 40 per cent has been assumed. A further improvement in the average annual output of shirts per operator for the industry will result from the elimination of many of the less efficient production units by merger or closure, and the probable doubling of the average company size in the next six years (12.1). A nominal 18 per cent (2½ per cent per year) has been allowed for this. It is likely that the shirt industry will follow the national trend towards a shorter working week; estimates of the further reductions are given in Table 13.2.

It is noticeable that in the shirt sector, which on average works 1 to 2 per cent longer hours than the clothing industry in general, the average hours have fallen at very much

Table 13.2 **Average hours worked per week**

Year	Male		Female	
	All manufacturing	*Shirts*	*All manufacturing*	*Shirts*
1960	44.7	44.2	40.5	39.5
1968	42.9	42.5	38.2	39.1
mid 1970s (estimate)	–	40	–	37

the same rate as in manufacturing industry as a whole. The future decline is expected to be less for women than for men, as the incentive for women to work will be increased with the pressure for a rising standard of living and as they become increasingly freed from domestic and home ties.

The demand for labour in the mid 1970s then is likely to work out as follows:

Table 13.3   **The changing labour requirements of the industry (percentages)**

	Current labour force (thousands)	*Increase due to higher output*	*Decrease due to higher productivity*	*Decrease due to improved processes*	*Increase due to shorter working week*	*Labour needs in the mid 1970s (thousands)*
Male	3.0				+6	2.5
		+35	−40	−18		
Female	34.0				+5	28.0
Total	37.0					30.5

There will thus be an overall reduction in the total labour force of between 15 and 20 per cent, the fall being slightly greater, proportionally, among female than male employees: by the mid 1970s the industry will be employing some 28,000 women and 2,500 men throughout the country.

The industry should not find that this reduction in its predominantly female labour force of some 3 per cent per year presents problems to either management or unions; the current annual turnover varies widely from company to company, although the average level is probably somewhat higher than that for clothing as a whole, which is around 50 per cent per year. With the increase of the school leaving age to 16 in 1973, there is certainly no overall danger of redundancy, although in certain localities the demand for suitable labour may fall, or for that matter rise, with the closure or expansion of a local shirt factory.

In *Your future in clothing*, it was estimated that average earnings in clothing would rise by some 30 per cent by 1973 and 70 per cent by 1978 over the 1968 level – an annual increase of about 5.5 per cent in real terms. The opportunities for profitable expansion open to the shirt industry appear to be rather greater than those facing much of the clothing trade; it is thus to be expected that the rate of increase in earnings will tend to be even higher than the above, especially as the nominal shirt operators' rates tend to be slightly below the average for clothing at the present (3.3).

The recommended technological developments (11.1) will produce a gradual but steady move towards a greater degree of automation, especially in the larger manufacturing units, which should enable increased productivity to be accompanied by improvements in wage levels. The shirt industry will, in fact, move into a position in which it can match its degree of automation to the availability and cost of labour. The adoption of many of the recommendations of the recent NBPI report on *Pay and Conditions in the clothing manufacturing industries* on standardisation of methods of proposing and agreeing wage rates, claims, etc, would help to promote the right balance of increased productivity, improved earnings and career prospects.

Strategic rather than tactical or short-term considerations should determine manpower policy, as the industry plans for a continuing well-paid and increasingly productive labour force to sustain its improved performance. Thus as labour becomes scarcer in the big cities and in the South-East, its greater availability in certain development areas should be an important factor in decisions to relocate production in say, Northern Ireland or the North-East.

Recruitment of operators, too, should be considered in a strategic sense, with an eye to their future in the industry. The recruitment procedure should include testing an applicant's abilities and passing her, if accepted, to a training school for a given period; here the Clothing Industry Training Board can give useful advice and financial help. After training, the operator should be matched to the job most suited to her, but, when an opportunity occurs, she should be retrained in further skills (and paid accordingly). Retraining can be facilitated by advanced teaching aids, such as auto operated audio/visual machines linked to sewing machines, which enable an operator to instruct herself in a new operation. The retraining policy has met with success in the USA because it makes any single operator in a flow line less indispensable and increases her versatility, a useful asset in a shirt factory. It also tends to improve management-labour relations by giving the operator a feeling of importance and, to some degree, security.

The advent of a small group of large companies will make possible joint training schemes, backed by the Training Board, in which companies of all sizes will take part. Their emphasis will be on training for a career in the industry rather than instruction in a limited range of skills, so that recruits will tend to remain longer than in the past, with consequent reduction of total training costs.

In addition to the normal machine operators and supervisors, the industry also needs a continuing supply of engineers and mechanics, who are at present in relatively short supply (11.2). It is suggested that a number of the larger companies should consider creating specific job opportunities for potential development engineers, possibly up to Higher National Certificate level and investigating, with the Training Board, the establishment of some recognised technical course, possibly on a day release basis, for such employees.

13.3 Management
Chapter 12 has made it plain that the reshaped structure of the UK shirt industry will require management skills which generally speaking it lacks at present. Three recommendations are made to remedy the deficiency.

Firstly, the industry should be prepared to buy in, from other industries and the professions, managerial expertise up to the highest level. As has been shown, present management is largely geared to controlling smaller establishments, relatively weak in professional qualifications, and inexperienced in modern techniques; there are likely to be few men now in the industry with the right skills for managing the large shirt companies of the future, and even at lower levels professional and managerial skills may have to be brought in. Fortunately, many of the skills required in, for example, financial control, corporate planning, marketing and personnel management do not demand an intimate knowledge of shirt manufacturing, although of course companies will still need men who understand the trade in all its aspects, and should continue to encourage shop floor supervisors to seek careers in management. The general aim in recruiting managers should be to acquire a wider blend of talents that will ensure a breadth of approach and an overall skill at management level. Attracting men of the right calibre will not be easy, particularly to some of the depressed areas of the North; but, correctly presented, the prospects of the shirt industry are bright enough to provide sufficiently promising careers.

A second method of obtaining management skill and expertise in the future will be by training, and it is recommended that much more is done to encourage it. The Training Board should be made aware of the interests of the shirt manufacturing companies in this direction, so that every use can be made of the many courses and seminars which are held regularly in many parts of the country. With outside assistance, from either the Training Board or appropriate consultants, effective 'in plant' training can be carried out. Senior executives should also be given experience of general management else-where, and a target provision of say 1 or 2 per cent of a manager's time, amounting to not more than some five days per year, would almost certainly pay dividends in creating an awareness and general appreciation of modern techniques. It is interesting to note that one of the other Training Boards in textiles has adopted a policy of offering assistance for management training schemes only to companies whose senior executive has himself recently taken part in some recognised management training; and a similar policy is judged appropriate for the shirt industry for the future.

Thirdly, the industry should support the proposals for a management training college made in the recent study of the strategic future of the wool textile industry, but extended to include the clothing industry as well as textiles. The subjects proposed for study by senior management are marketing (including market research), long range company planning, computer applications, management controls, management and cost accountancy, operations research, production and stock control, critical path programming and personnel management. All are relevant to the clothing industry in general and to the shirt industry in particular, and the shirt industry is strongly recommended to take up the proposal with the clothing and textile industries.

Appendix A   Definitions of retail outlets

The definitions of the retail outlets as used in this report, and in particular Figure 4.1 and Table 4.2 are as follows:

Chain stores: large multiple organisations selling a range of merchandise: eg Marks and Spencer, Littlewoods, British Home Stores, Woolworths.

Department stores: large multi-product outlets.

Independents: independent outfitters — organisations selling a range of garments with fewer than 10 outlets.

independent tailors — organisations specialising in men's outerwear, particularly suits, with fewer than 10 outlets.

Multiples: multiple outfitters — organisations selling a range of garments with more than 10 outlets.

multiple tailors — organisations specialising in men's outerwear, particularly suits, with more than 10 outlets.

Mail order: warehousing companies selling shirts through the mail.

Co-operative societies: multi-product, multiple outlets in which the customer can buy a non-negotiable share of the equity.

Others: market stalls

supermarkets

wholesale warehouse — customers supplied at discount prices on a cash and carry basis from the warehouse.

Appendix B   Detail of representative shirt definitions

Commodity shirt

Fabric:	Minimum iron cotton, white or plain colour, 122 x 70 weave, 4.5 oz/sq yd or warp knit nylon 6.4 yd/lb at 36 inch width
Cloth content:	27 yd per dozen shirts at 36 inch width (gross)
Buttons:	Low grade white polyester, 10d per gross
Thread:	Cotton, 60/3 fold
Style:	Stitched collar, french plain front, long sleeves, and single, button cuff
Construction:	Collar – bonded fabric lining with one fusible patch, lock stitched with no back tack
	front – single turn, unlined with limited stitching of button holes
	body – double yoke, tail and seams overlocked, sleeve guard – and lock stitched on continuous facing
	cuffs – single, square, button cuff with bonded or cheap woven lining

Medium-quality shirt

Fabric:	Polyester/cotton 67/33 blend, permanent press finish, 90 x 82 weave, 3.6 oz/sq yd
Cloth content:	29 yd per dozen shirt at 36 inch width (gross)
Buttons:	Non staining coloured polyester, 72d per gross
Thread:	Cotton or polyester/cotton, 80/3 fold
Style:	Stitched or bluff edge collar, limited permutation of fronts, cuffs and collar, full bodied
Construction:	Collar – zero shrunk, bias cut lining and 4 fusible patches (of sintered type permanent press)
	front – french front, or fly front with additional strap of fabric with lightweight sanforised interlining
	body – double (two piece) yoke, seams overlocked, tail hemmed and top stitched
	sleeve gauntlet – stitched on piece, other side hemmed
	cuffs – single cuff link or button fastening or double cuff with link fastening, laminated fusible lining or zero shrunk drip dry

Specialist shirt

Fabric:	Best Sea Island cotton woven
Cloth content:	31 yd per dozen shirts at 36 inch width (gross)
Buttons:	Best quality coloured and sculpted polyester 120d per gross
Thread:	140/3 fold cotton or cotton/nylon blend
Style:	Variety of styles in various sleeve lengths

Construction: Collar: swiss two-fold yarn woven lining at 9 oz/sq yd bias cut, with best fusible patches, various styles

front — lined front, various styles

body — gusset tails, hemmed and topstitched, 3 piece yoke.

sleeve gauntlet — stitched on piece, other side hemmed, top stitched with run back stitching

cuffs — mitred single cuff with link or button fastening, or double cuff with link fastening, laminated lining of high quality 10 oz/sq yd weight.

Appendix C Discounted cash flow (DCF) return

When evaluating the profitability of a new project the industry usually uses the criterion of return on net assets, before tax.

Table C1 illustrates how this is done:

Table C1 Calculation of return on net assets

Investment required at beginning of project	£100,000
Income over 4 year life of project	£133,000
Net profit over 4 year life (£133,000–£100,000)	£ 33,000
Annual net profit $\dfrac{£33,000}{4}$	£ 8,250
Average net assets $\dfrac{£100,000}{2}$	£ 50,000
Return on net assets $\dfrac{£8,250 \times 100}{50,000}$	16.5%

The calculation in Table C1 takes no account of when, during the project life, the income occurs. The capital invested in the project has to be serviced until it is recovered. If the bulk of the income comes in the third and fourth years the project will be less attractive than if most of the income arises in the first two years; this is because in the former case there is a slower recovery of capital and, hence, a higher capital service charge. It has been assumed that the total investment is written off after four years.

To take account of the timing of receipts and payments, the discounted cash flow (DCF) rate of return is now widely used to evaluate new projects. A project's DCF rate of return is the maximum rate of interest that can be paid to finance the project and yet break even, provided capital can be repaid at will. This can be illustrated by a simple example: if, for the project illustrated in Table C1, the income in each of the four years was £10,000 (Year 1), £30,000 (Year 2), £38,000 (Year 3) and £55,000 (Year 4), the DCF rate of return would be 10 per cent per year; on the other hand, had the income for each of the four years been £55,000, £38,000, £30,000 and £10,000, the rate of return would be approximately 16.25 per cent per year. Table C2 shows how these DCF rates of return are calculated.

The DCF rate of return — as its name implies — is based on cash flows, not accounting profits. One of the important items in any profitable company's cash flows is taxation and as every company is aiming to maximise its profits available for distribution to its shareholders, this means maximising post-tax profits. The extra Corporation Tax that will have to be paid as a result of a new project should therefore be included in the evaluation: it is a simple matter, using DCF, to adjust the cash flows for Corporation Tax.

(In practice the DCF rate of return is found by systematically trying different rates of return until the one is found that makes the project break even).

Table C2   Calculation of DCF return

Year	Beginning of year outstanding £	Interest for year at 10 per cent pa £	Cash income £	End of year outstanding £
10 per cent pa DCF rate of return				
1	100,000	10,000	(10,000)	100,000
2	100,000	10,000	(30,000)	80,000
3	80,000	8,000	(38,000)	50,000
4	50,000	5,000	(55,000)	—

Year	Beginning of year outstanding £	Interest for year at 16.25 per cent pa £	Cash income £	End of year outstanding £
16.25 per cent pa DCF rate of return				
1	100,000	16,251	(55,000)	61,251
2	61,251	9,954	(38,000)	33,205
3	33,205	5,397	(30,000)	8,602
4	8,602	1,398	(10,000)	—

Several computer bureaux offer a simple programming service that takes the tedium out of the calculations, and enables a large number of alternatives to be evaluated cheaply and accurately. Furthermore, an electronic device specifically designed for making DCF has recently been developed under licence agreement with the NRDC.

Appendix D   Return on net assets: equivalent in DCF terms

When evaluating new capital projects, the industry should look for a return on net assets employed (before Corporation Tax) of about 20 per cent per year. This is, of course, a very broad yardstick, and the return being looked for should obviously vary from company to company and, maybe, from project to project. Since this criterion of return on net assets employed does not take into account Corporation Tax or the timing of cash flows, a typical investment of £2,000 that gives rise to a 20 per cent per year return on net assets has been taken, so as to calculate the equivalent DCF rate of return, after Corporation Tax. This is shown in Table D1.

A number of assumptions have been made:

(a)   The total investment of £2,000 is split equally between fixed and working capital.

(b)   The fixed capital investment of £1,000 is split between plant and buildings in the ratio 40:60.

(c)   The working capital requirement is built up over 2 years of operation, 75 per cent in the first year and 25 per cent in the second.

(d)   The project is in a non-development area of the UK and therefore qualifies for a 20 per cent investment grant on plant.

(e)   The plant has a life of eight years and that at the end of the eight years the value of the buildings is equivalent to their written down value for tax purposes.

(f)   The plant is written off in the books over 8 years and the buildings over 15. Both are depreciated on a 'straight-line' basis.

(g)   For tax purposes, the plant qualifies for a 15 per cent writing down allowance on a 'declining balance' basis; on buildings there is a 15 per cent initial allowance and 4 per cent writing down allowance, on a 'straight-line' basis.

(h)   The company is in a tax-paying position.

(i)   The project achieves full profitability in the 4th year of operation and the building up is as shown in Table D2.

The right-hand column of Table D1 shows the net cash flows resulting from the project. These are the totals of the fixed and working capital investments, the investment grants, the cash value of the taxation depreciation allowances and the net earnings. The DCF rate of return on these cash flows is 10 per cent per year.

In calculating the capital charges for the international cost comparison, the cost of servicing capital has therefore been taken as 10 per cent per year, after Corporation Tax, calculated on a DCF basis.

Table D1 Relationship of return on net assets to DCF rate of return

| | Fixed capital | | | Investment grant | Book depreciation | Taxation depreciation | | | | Earnings for 20 per cent return on net assets | | Net cash flow |
| | Buildings | Plant | Working capital | | | Building | Plant | Total | Net at 45 per cent | Gross | Net of tax at 45 per cent | |
Year	£	£	£	£	£	£	£	£	£	£	£	£
0	(600)	(400)										(1,000)
1			(750)	80	80	114	48	162		160	160	(510)
2			(250)		80	24	41	65	73	280	208	31
3					80	24	35	59	29	360	234	263
4					80	24	29	53	27	400	238	265
5					80	24	25	49	24	400	220	244
6					80	24	21	45	22	400	220	242
7					80	24	18	42	20	400	220	240
8	318		1,000		42	24	103	127	19	400	220	1,557
9									57		(180)	(123)
	(282)	(400)	0	80	602	282	320	602	271	2,800	1,540	1,209

Table D2 Return on net assets employed

Year	Level of profits End of year — per cent	Average for year — per cent
1	50	25
2	75	65.5
3	100	87.5
4 onwards	100	100

The return on net assets employed (before tax) has been calculated as follows:

	£	£
Working capital		1,000
Fixed capital	1,000	
Less: Investment grant	80	
	920	
Less: 50% of book depreciation	301	619
Average net capital employed		1,619
Cash earnings in years of full profitability		400
Less: Annual book depreciation		80
Annual profits		320
Return on net assets employed		20 per cent pa

Appendix E   International costs of finance

Fixed capital

In the case of operating costs, it is possible to arrive at annual figures and then convert them to a cost per shirt. Capital costs do not, of course, occur annually, so it is necessary to calculate an equivalent annual cost that is sufficient to:

(1)   Write off the investment over its economic life

(2)   Provide for enough profit so that an adequate return on the capital employed is obtained.

(3)   Allow for the taxation that must be paid on the profit

(4)   Allow for investment grants

(5)   Allow for the period of build-up to full profitability during the early years of the life of the investment.

Capital factors have therefore been calculated for each country. These have been applied to the capital costs of plant and buildings to convert them to equivalent annual figures.

To calculate a capital factor it is necessary to set out the cash flows that stem from a typical investment of a given amount — £1,000 has been taken — and then find the annual profit that will provide for all the items listed above. This annual figure is then expressed as a percentage of the original investment — £1,000 — to arrive at the capital factor.

Different capital factors have been calculated for each country; these vary with the different systems of taxation and investment grants. The fiscal data for each country is set out in Table E3.

Table E1   Capital factors for fixed capital

Country	Capital factor (r) per cent	Index
UK Non-development area	24.3	100
UK development area	18.1	74.5
UK — Northern Ireland	14.4	59.3
Eire — export	22.3	91.8
Eire — home market	26.7	109.9
West Germany	25.0	102.9
Portugal	23.8	97.9
Italy	27.5	113.2
Hong Kong	21.4	88.1
USA	30.1	123.9

Because of the difficulty in obtaining the detailed data, and because the shirt industry is not 'fixed-capital-intensive', a number of parameters have been assumed as constant in the different countries. The common assumptions are as follows:

The commissioning period for new capital investment is one year or less.

That 60 per cent of the capital cost of a factory lies in the building, and 40 per cent in the plant and equipment.

Investment in plant has an 8 year economic life, with no terminal value at the end of its its life; buildings have a resale value equivalent to their tax written down value after 8 years.

The build-up during the first three years to full profitability is as set out in Appendix D.

There is a one year delay in the payment of tax and the receipt of investment grants, where applicable.

The cost of servicing capital is 10 per cent per year after Corporation Tax, calculated on a DCF basis.

Table E2 Capital factors for working capital

Country	Capital factors (r) per cent	Scaling factors
UK	16.8	1.042
Eire – export	11.0	1.028
Eire – home market	18.2	1.046
West Germany	14.7	1.037
Portugal	13.8	1.035
Italy	18.1	1.045
Hong Kong	11.5	1.029
USA	19.8	1.050

The capital factors for fixed capital in the different countries are set out below; they are also shown as index numbers with the base case of the UK non-development area set as 100. In Eire, profits on exports are exempt from tax; different capital factors have therefore been calculated for their home market and for exports.

Table E4 shows how the capital factor for the non-development area of the UK has been calculated. The other capital factors have been arrived at in a similar way.

Working capital
Working capital is not eligible for investment grants or taxation allowances, nor does it have to be written off but it does have to be serviced out of profits that have borne Corporation Tax. Capital factors for working capital have been calculated for each country.

Since the level of working capital is a function of activity, a factor has been calculated for each country for scaling up the operating costs to take into account the cost of working capital. This scaling factor is made up by

$$1 + \frac{1}{W} \cdot r, \text{ where } \frac{1}{W} = \text{relationship of the average level of total working capital to annual operating costs.}$$

r = capital factor for working capital

Table E3   Fiscal data for different countries

Country	Tax on profits	Investment grants — Plant %	Investment grants — Buildings %	Depreciation allowances Initial — Plant %	Initial — Buildings %	Annual — Plant %	Annual — Buildings %
UK non-development area	Corporation tax at 45%	20	–	–	15	15 DB	4 SL
UK development area	Corporation tax at 45%	40	25	–	15	15 DB	4 SL
UK Northern Ireland	Corporation tax at 45%	45	45	–	15	15 DB	4 SL
Eire	Exports bear no tax. 50% on internal sales	–	–	50	20	5 SL	2 SL
West Germany	Different rates, depending on whether or not profits are distributed. Assuming 60% of profits are distributed, corporation tax averages at 34.3%	–	–	5	5	10 SL	4 SL
Portugal	Industrial tax — 18%, local taxes of 17.5% and commerce and industry tax of 48.6% of this amount. An additional complementary tax on distributed profits gives a total gross amount of 31.2%	–	–	–	–	22.5 DB	4.5 SL
Italy	36% (inc. local rates and surcharges) plus approximately 14% company tax = 50%	–	–	–	–	10 SL + 40% accelerated depreciation spread over 4 years	
Hong Kong	Profits tax at 15%	–	–	20	20	10 DB	4 SL
USA	22% on first $25,000 profits, thereafter profits are taxed at 48%, all subject to a 10% surcharge. Additional state taxes between 5% and 10% increase rate to 55%	–	–	–	–	15 DB	3 SL

Note: DB = Declining balance
SL = Straight line

Table E4 Calculation of capital factor for fixed capital in UK non-development area

Year	Gross capital Plant £	Gross capital Buildings £	Investment grant Plant £	Tax allowances Plant £	Tax allowances Buildings £	Tax allowances Total £	Tax allowances Net value £	Profit Gross £	Profit Net £	Discount factors at 10 per cent pa £	Net present value Investment £	Net present value Profit £
0	(400)	(600)								1.000	1000	
1			80	48	114	162		0.250x	0.250x	.909	(73)	0.227x
2				41	24	65	73	0.625x	0.513x	.826	(60)	0.424x
3				35	24	59	29	0.875x	0.594x	.751	(22)	0.446x
4				29	24	53	27	1.000x	0.606x	.683	(18)	0.414x
5				25	24	49	24	1.000x	0.550x	.621	(15)	0.342x
6				21	24	45	22	1.000x	0.550x	.564	(12)	0.310x
7				18	24	42	20	1.000x	0.550x	.513	(10)	0.282x
8		318		103	24	127	19	1.000x	0.550x	.467	(157)	0.257x
9							57		(0.450x)	.424	(24)	(0.191x)
	(400)	(282)	80	320	282	602	271	6.750x	3.713x		609	2.511x

$$x = \frac{609}{2.511} = 242.53 \quad r = 24.3\%$$

The broad assumption has been made that total working capital is one-quarter of annual operating costs. The capital factors for working capital and the scaling factors are set out in Table E2.

Table E5 shows how the capital factor for working capital in the non-development area of the UK has been calculated. The other factors have been arrived at in a similar way.

Table E5   Calculation of capital factor for working capital in UK

Year	Working capital £	Profit Gross £	Profit Net £	Discount factors at 10 per cent £	Net present value Investment £	Net present value Profit £
1	(750)	0.250x	0.250x	.909	682	0.277x
2	(250)	0.625x	0.513x	.826	206	0.424x
3		0.875x	0.594x	.751		0.446x
4		1.000x	0.606x	.683		0.414x
5		1.000x	0.550x	.621		0.342x
6		1.000x	0.550x	.564		0.310x
7		1.000x	0.550x	.513		0.282x
8	1000	1.000x	0.550x	.467	(467)	0.257x
9			(0.450x)	.424		(0.191x)
		6.750x	3.713x		421	2.511x

$$x = \frac{421}{2.511} = 167.66 \quad r = 16.8\%$$

Appendix F Statistics on UK market size and production

Table F1 Statistics on UK market size and production

	1960	1961	1962	1963	1964	1965	1966	1967	1968	1969
Volume of shirt sales in the UK (million units) (best estimate)	53.0	52.0	52.0	57.0	64.3	65.0	67.0	67.8	75.0	71.
Value of UK shirt sales (£ million real value) (best estimate)	94.5	96.9	93.6	110.0	122	130	134	128	140	138
Volume of UK shirt production (million units)	39.6	41.3	39.6	44.2	47.3	52.8	54.6	53.0	56.9	54.
Value of UK shirt production (£ million real value)										
retail sales in UK	84.6	87.0	81.8	94.2	102	117	120	111	116	115
home consumption at manufacturers selling prices	50.6	51.2	49.0	56.4	61.2	70.2	71.9	65.5	69.5	68.
home production at manufacturers selling prices	51.6	52.2	50.1	57.7	62.8	72.0	73.9	68.0	72.5	72.

All information in this table is also shown graphically in Figures 1.1, 1.2, 2.1, 2.2.

Printed in England for Her Majesty's Stationery Office
By McCorquodale Printers Ltd., London

H.M. 3911 Dd. 500377 K22 9/70 McC. 3309.